Gifted Children

Gifted Children

How to Identify and
Teach Them

Owenita Sanderlin

Revised by Ruthe Rose Lundy

South Brunswick and New York: A. S. Barnes and Company
London: Thomas Yoseloff Ltd

Also by Owenita Sanderlin:

Jeanie O'Brien

Johnny

Creative Teaching

Teaching Gifted Children

Tennis Rebel

© 1979 by A. S. Barnes and Co., Inc.

A. S. Barnes and Co., Inc.
Cranbury, New Jersey 08512

Thomas Yoseloff Ltd.
Magdalen House
136-148 Tooley Street
London SE1 2TT, England

Library of Congress Cataloging in Publication Data

Sanderlin, Owenita.
    Gifted children.

    Edition of 1973 published under title: Teaching gifted children.
    Bibliography: p.
    Includes index.
    1. Gifted children--Education.   I. Lundy, Ruthe Rose, 1922-
II. Title.
LC3993.S23   371.9'5   79-50768
ISBN 0-498-02328-1

Printed in the United States of America

To
Cecil Munsey and David Hermanson
for all their help and kindness.

Contents

Acknowledgments

The authors of the original and the revision of this text are most grateful for the generous assistance and encouragement of Dr. David P. Hermanson, Coordinator of the Gifted Programs of the San Diego Unified School District and to Dr. Cecil Munsey, who at the time of the original writing was a Resource Teacher for the San Diego Schools. They provided resources and documents which proved most valuable. To the teachers and parents and school staffs of the San Diego and the Palo Alto school districts, special thanks are extended. Their wisdom and expertise were an important part of the ideas developed. They represent a standard of excellence which results from deep commitment and caring for all children and this includes the gifted.

Anyone involved with the education of the gifted must acknowledge the contributions and inspiration that has come over the years from such people as John Curtis Gowan, Ruth Martinson, E. Paul Torrance, James Gallagher, Bill Vassar, Paul Plowman, Walter Barbe, J. P. Guilford, Maurice Freehill and many, many others.

A special note of thanks goes to friends and colleagues of the "revisor"—John Martin (Boss), Dick Carey, Rosemarie Moore and Betty Rogaway.

For the photographs, we wish to thank Professor E. Paul Torrance of the University of Georgia, Dr. Cecil Munsey and Dr. David Hermanson of the San Diego Unified School District, Dr. William Vassar of the Connecticut State Department of Education, Joan Targ and Patricia Robinson of the Palo Alto Unified School District, Dr. Julian Stanley of Johns Hopkins University, Arthur Gatty of the Pennsylvania Governor's School for the Arts at Bucknell University, and Charlene R. Duncan of the Wichita, Kansas Public Schools.

An Introduction to the Controversy
What Is It; Why Is It?

Why is there controversy about education for the gifted? Why are proponents of special planning for the gifted often challenged? Why are so few dollars spent on the education of the gifted?

Is education for the gifted undemocratic?

Who are the gifted? What is an IQ? How valid is it? Can it be changed? Is the IQ concept of giftedness outmoded? Of what use is the knowledge of a child's IQ score?

Is intelligence chiefly hereditary? How much can it be affected by the environment?

Are children of superior intelligence likely to be emotionally disturbed? Physically weak?

Are bright children bored in our schools?

What can parents do? How much say should they have in their own children's education? Can parents and teachers develop more gifted children through infant and early childhood education?

Should children be grouped by age? Ability? Grouped at all?

Should children who are capable of learning faster be accelerated in school? If so, how?

What about enrichment?

How should gifted children be taught? What makes a "gifted" teacher?

How much can we afford to do for the gifted? Where do we get the money? Can better education for the gifted lead to improvements in the education of all children?

These questions have been asked for so many generations that we wonder if they will ever be answered, although at the present moment there is a new hope—lately the word dream has come into respectable use—that they will.

Never before in the history of public education has it been more important to teach responsibly—that is, to be responsive to the individual needs of the students of the current generation. To teach responsibly is to teach the skills and to develop abilities in young people that will enable them to function effectively in their world—a world that is beautiful, rewarding, and soul-satisfying and yet a world full of dangers, poverty of body and spirit, and potential destruction of environment and persons.

To teach responsibly we must give every student equal opportunity to discover and develop his unique potential. It is imperative that parents and educators be aware of the uniqueness of all youngsters and groups of youngsters. This book could have been written about educationally handicapped children, children of less than average intelligence, those who are emotionally disturbed, or those who make average progress through school. The task would have been a worthy one. Of equal rank on the list of our responsibilities, if we truly believe in personalizing instruction, is to attend to the uniqueness of youngsters who have the ability to learn rapidly and easily. Writing this book, therefore, is also worthy and must be done.

In the 1770s Americans pioneered a new freedom in government; in the 1970s leaders are pioneering a new freedom in education. Gifted teachers, administrators, and students will have much to do with the success of the necessary experimentation that must precede any worthwhile change. Throughout history the creative thinkers, the gifted leaders, have been the pioneers, not only because of their physical courage but because they have had the intellectual courage to try something that has never been done before.

We don't have all the answers yet to the controversy that exists regarding teaching the gifted, but before we can make any widespread changes we have to listen to the debate, and note that even the authorities disagree! Unfortunately, no matter how exciting and successful a new kind of schooling turns out to be, it is too often buried under an avalanche of uninformed or emotionally charged community criticism. The community must be a part of any deliberation and implementation of educational change. Schools and families working together toward common goals are an unbeatable combination.

So, let us begin by discussing those questions everybody asks, and then go on to describe some of the experiences gifted students are having, what can be done for our most able students, why it should be done, and how it will help all students, everywhere.

Professor E. Paul Torrance checks out his well-known theories on creativity with children in Georgia. (Photo Courtesy of Dr. Torrance)

Gifted Children

1
Who Are The Gifted?
How Do We Know One
When We See One?

Issues:

Why are there different definitions for giftedness?
What does gifted really mean?
Are there limitations of giftedness?
What is the relationship between giftedness and creativeness?
Can a child who scores below the gifted range "act gifted?"

ALFRED BINET (co-originator, in 1905, of the individual intelligence tests still most widely used to determine IQ—intelligence quotient): *. . . a father and mother who raise a child themselves, who watch over him and study him fondly, would have great satisfaction in knowing that the intelligence of a child can be measured, and would willingly make the effort to find out if their own child is intelligent.*

ARTHUR JENSEN (1969): [*The Binet-Simon intelligence test*]*is now regarded as one of the major "breakthroughs" in the history of psychology.*

JOHN CURTIS GOWAN and GEORGE DEMOS (1964): *A value judgment must be made by the school district on . . . what it means by a "gifted child."*

WILLARD ABRAHAM (educator and writer, 1958): *We cannot and should not tell a parent an exact IQ. The reason is simple—there is no such thing.*

17

THE EDITORS OF *THE ATLANTIC* (September 1971): *IQ tests and their like have become controversial, in spite of the hundreds of millions of them still given around the world. . .lately in America . . .public discussion of intelligence requires physical not to mention intellectual courage, for the subject is close to taboo.*

ARTHUR JENSEN (1969): *Had the first IQ tests been devised in a hunting culture, "general intelligence" might well have turned out to involve visual acuity and running speed rather than vocabulary and symbol manipulation.*

JOHN CURTIS GOWAN (in a speech in San Diego, January 31, 1972): *IQ giftedness is an outmoded concept.*

JOAN BECK (*Chicago Tribune* staff journalist, columnist, and mother, 1967): *In one research project, in which the I.Q.'s of 152 children were tested repeatedly between the ages of twenty-one months and eighteen years, two youngsters showed increases of 70 and 79 points.* [see Honzik, in Bibliography.] *This is enough difference to move a youngster from the general classification of "educable mentally retarded" to "gifted." The scores of two other youngsters in this long-term study group decreased about the same amount. . . .One changed as much as 50 points and several as much as 30 points between the ages of six and eight. . . .Similar changes in children's I.Q.s have been noted in many other research studies, particularly when youngsters under age six are involved.*

PHILIP VERNON (*In Psychology and Education of Gifted Children,* 1977): *Certain children are gifted chiefly in some special area or type of ability rather than being all rounders with high I.Q.s.*

RUTH MARTINSON (from her research summary compiled for the U.S. Office of Education, in the Report to Congress, *Education of the Gifted and Talented,* Vol. 2, 1971): *Identification of the gifted and talented in different parts of the country has been piecemeal, sporadic, and sometimes nonexistent. . . .Special injustice has occurred through apathy toward certain minorities, although neglect of the gifted in this country is a universal and increasing problem.*

J. P. GUILFORD (psychologist noted for his work on the structure of the intellect, in *The Gifted Child Quarterly* 6, 1962): . . . *selection on the basis of IQ alone will definitely miss many potentially gifted children. . . . .Although about 60 primary intellectual abilities have now been demonstrated, the number of these for which there are available tests is much smaller.*

E. PAUL TORRANCE (in *The Gifted Child Quarterly* 12, 1968): *. . . if one uses only an intelligence test and therefore identifies the upper twenty percent as gifted, he would miss seventy percent of those who would be identified as falling in the top twenty percent on tests of creative thinking ability.*

FRANK RIESSMAN (professor and author of noted books in sociology, 1968): *We've neglected the huge pool of gifted individuals among the poor. This is not a few people—thousands of people in the disadvantaged and ghetto are being screened out.*

WILLARD ABRAHAM (1968): *The emphases on individualized instruction, behavioral objectives and programmed learning and computer-managed instruction . . . all that brings us far from the gobbledygook of superficial enrichment, identification and definition of who is talented or gifted of a few years ago.*[1]

[1]. The statements of Mr. Riessman and Mr. Abraham were contributed to Charles Bish's "What's New in Education for the Gifted," *Accent on Talent* 2 (1968).

SIDNEY P. MARLAND, JR. (Definition of "gifted and talented" established by the advisory panel for the Commissioner of Education pursuant to Public Law 91-230, Section 806, for purposes of federal education programs in the 1971 Report to Congress): *Gifted and talented children are those identified by professionally qualified persons who by virtue of outstanding abilities, are capable of high performance. These are children who require differentiated educational programs and/or services beyond those normally provided by the regular school program in order to realize their contribution to self and society.*

Children capable of high performance include those with demonstrated achievement and/or potential ability in any of the following areas, singly or in combination:

1. general intellectual ability

2. specific academic aptitude

3. *creative or productive thinking*
4. *leadership ability*
5. *visual and performing arts*
6. *psychomotor ability*

CECIL MUNSEY (Writer, teacher in *Programs for the Gifted Bulletin*, Spring 1971): *A recent national survey by the U.S. Office of Education has revealed that 57 percent of the nation's schools claim they don't have any gifted children.*

Ricky Ponce de Leon is a musical genius. He is reported to have an IQ of 55. Yet he plays the organ and the piano, guitar, and several other instruments, has composed many songs, and knows about 1,000 songs by heart. At nineteen he gave organ concerts in Los Angeles, San Francisco, and Sacramento, and he played in a nightclub in Manila, his hometown.

Anne Sullivan, who was later to become Helen Keller's teacher, was beaten by her parents and sent to a poorhouse after their death; almost blind herself, she could not read or write until she was sent to Perkins Institute for the Blind; by fifteen she was teaching Greek history to a class of ten-year-olds. Her gift for teaching is legendary now.

Who are the gifted? It is sometimes hard to tell.

A mother I know was puzzled by her only child, born when the mother was almost forty. She soon suspected that he was not mentally retarded, as some people thought, but it took her over three years to establish the fact that he was actually a gifted child. Later tests revealed that he was highly gifted, with an IQ above 170.

A young friend, Mark Hodes, highly talented in teaching mathematics to "creative mathematicians, not just good bookkeepers," cautions us to beware of what he calls "the sleeping sponge syndrome." He says, "Unfortunately, it is difficult to distinguish between a sleeping sponge and a stone. A child who never volunteers a response may, nevertheless, be a gifted child."

John Curtis Gowan and George Demos in *The Education and Guidance of the Ablest* (511 pages) — include the following figures on above-average ability in terms of the Stanford-Binet IQ. Other tests yield so-called IQs that vary from these norms, but the Stanford-Binet has been the most widely accepted scale for over fifty years:

a. *The academically talented:* above 115 IQ (16 percent of population).

b. *The superior:* above 125 IQ (5 percent of population).

c. *The gifted* (Terman's use): above 140 IQ (0.6 percent of population).

d. *The highly gifted:* above 160 IQ (0.007 percent of population).

Thus, the highly gifted would be one of seventy or fewer persons per million; an amusing example these authors cite is an eighteen-month-old baby who could beat his parents at double solitaire. (You might try this game if you just cannot wait to find out if your child is a genius!)

Thomas and Crescimbeni's helpful paperback, *Guiding the Gifted Child*, tabulates the following statistics based on a population of 200 million:

below 60 IQ, *trainable:* .6 percent (1.2 million people).

60-69 IQ, *educable:* 2.0 percent (4 million people).

70-79 IQ, *very slow learners and high educables:* 5.6 percent (11.2 million people).

80-89 IQ, *low average or slow learners:* 14.5 percent (29 million people).

90-99 IQ, *average learners:* 23 percent (46 million people).

100-109 IQ, *average learners:* 23.5 percent (47 million people).

110-119 IQ, *high average, bright, and fast learners:* 18.1 percent (36.2 million people).

120-129 IQ, *superior:* 8.2 percent (16.4 million people).

130-139 IQ, *gifted to highly gifted:* 3.1 percent (6.2 million people).

140 IQ or above, *highly gifted to genius:* 1.0-1.5 percent (2 million to 3 million people).

These authors conclude that one in a million individuals may have an IQ of 180. Parents of these most highly gifted children (180-200) are sometimes told, "The scale didn't go high enough to measure your child."

Should parents be told their child's IQ? Traditionally, the great majority of educators say no, but, as may be noted in the controversy at the beginning of this chapter, there is a highly regarded and intelligent minority who say parents should be told. Probably, if you are reading this book, and your child is gifted, you'll know it! As to the "exact" IQ, that may vary; and the parent who has been given a figure may be tempted to compare notes with other parents, sometimes with painful social results for the child. So if you do know the "awe-ful truth," as I for one believe you have a right to know, it is better to keep it to yourself.

Teachers are usually given access to this information when it is available; of course the expense of individual testing means that many children, particularly those who do not seem especially bright or especially slow, never get tested for IQ, unless their parents arrange to have it done themselves. Occasionally, this is a good idea, if only for the parents' own peace of mind.

When one child in the family is gifted—and studies have shown that this child is frequently the oldest—parents sometimes expect too much of their other children; to be sure, it is common for more than one child in a family to be gifted, and in some cases a parent may overlook a younger gifted or talented child. Psychologists emphatically agree that intelligence can be measured, so IQ tests can help parents avoid expecting too much or too little of each individual child in the family.

It is often said that teachers overlook gifted children because they are shy on the one hand, or badly behaved on the other. However, authorities agree that highly intelligent students, as a rule, compare favorably with the general population socially and emotionally as well as physically. Ordinarily, the gifted child stands out in the crowd; you can not miss him—or her—whether or not you know his IQ. Some people, unfortunately, feel that such children *should* be ignored—"for their own sakes."

The 1971 Report to Congress, quoted above, states in no uncertain terms that they should *not* be ignored—for all our sakes.

The first step toward developing the talents of our children is to find them as early as possible. Ever since Alfred Binet, at the turn of this century, found a way to test mental ability, we have been using his tests, as revised by Lewis Terman of Stanford University, and similar tests to give a numerical score to the intelligence of school children.

Binet's original motive for working the tests out with his colleague Theodore Simon in France had nothing to do with "gifted" students.

He was concerned with vindicating falsely labeled "retarded" children who, solely on the basis of opinion and guesswork, were denied an education. Imagine the indignation of an American parent if he were told his child was not smart enough to go to school, and his relief when tests were devised by which mental ability could be *proved*. Also, in cases where children actually are retarded, it is a good thing to know to what extent, what can be expected of them, and what kind of education they should have.

Although special education for the retarded at two levels (the trainable below 50 and the educable at about 75 and below) outnumber special gifted programs in the United States, (from about 1916 on), a natural interest in the children who scored high on these tests led to the establishment of a numerical definition of mental giftedness. Professor Terman's study of 1,000 California children of 140 IQ and above is probably the most fascinating and complete follow-up of any group of human beings over such a long period of time (*Genetic Studies of Genius* [Stanford, Calif.: Stanford University Press, 1925, 1926, 1930, 1947, 1959]—see Bibliography for volume titles).

But any cutoff score on intelligence tests will exclude many children with high potential as creative thinkers, leaders, athletic champions (the Greeks never called *their* athletes dumb!), mechanical geniuses, mentally or physically handicapped musicians or artists, and an assortment of other potentially outstanding citizens who can not fulfill all the tasks on the tests.

These tasks include memory (repeat five numbers, forward and backward, or sentences), logic (fold and cut a paper and tell how many holes will be in it without unfolding it), vocabulary, reading and reading comprehension, rhyming words, and drawing or fitting geometrical forms, to mention a few. Since school districts and states that have special programs for the gifted often require the child to have a certain score, which varies from 116 to 140 or higher in different localities, boys and girls with outstanding talents are often left out.

This is compounded by the fact that unrecognized but common physical disabilities, such as partial deafness, petit mal, or eye disorders, would affect scores on any test. Emotional upsets on the day of testing on the part of either testee or tester, lack of discipline or concentration, inefficient testers are among the many things that can deny a child who *is* gifted his right to profit by education especially designed for him. He needs it even more than does the child who is good at passing intelligence tests and influencing teachers by a pleasant personality and by posing no problems.

But—let there be no question about this—it is not possible to do well on these tests without exceptional mental ability. Studies have been made that find that while study or coaching may raise a score 10 or 15 points at most, this is about the same "spread" that we get in testing the same child on different days; this varies for physical, emotional, and other reasons, such as rapport with the tester.

An understandable human reaction occurs when a bright boy or girl who does consistently good work in school is denied the privilege of being in a gifted group. One frustrated mother had a daughter who kept testing at 128, even when tests were repeated; the cutoff score was 132.

"Some day you'll know how it feels to have a gifted child that nobody can identify!" this mother told the young lady psychologist who tested her daughter the third time.

That is a funny story, but if one thinks about it, one does not laugh. An IQ of 128 indicates superior mental ability, and combined with industry and desire, that girl could handle the work in a gifted program better than a pupil with an IQ of 160 if he or she were not industrious or interested. If I could have my pick of children to bring up or teach, generally speaking I would choose the ones with IQs between about 120 and 140. Other teachers agree that they are usually a joy. But one should not "put down" the geniuses, either.

Just as we should aim at including the less easily identified "disadvantaged" children who have gifts to offer our democracy, so should we try to include *all* the bright children who would benefit by the freedom and stimulation of special education for the "deprived" gifted, not just some of them.

What about those "creative" kids we have been excluding? As Professor Torrance says, hundreds of studies, like those of Jacob Getzels and Philip Jackson in 1962, have shown that 70 percent of the children who score in the top 20 percent on tests of creative thinking ability will not be identified as gifted (in the top 20 percent) on the basis of intelligence tests. Creativity, then, is not the same *kind* of intellectual ability as that measured by the traditional mental tests; but certainly it is a function, and one of a very high order indeed, of the mind.

During the past two decades interest in creativity has flourished. J. P. Guilford's famous cubic model of "the structure of the intellect" (1961) led to the fascinating "Williams Cube" (see Frank E. Williams, "Models for Encouraging Creativity in the Classroom," *Educational Technology Magazine*, December 1969, reprinted in Gowan and Torrance's *Educating the Ablest*, 1971).

E. Paul Torrance of Georgia, Al Hatch of Los Angeles, and George Witt, working with disadvantaged students in New Haven, Connecticut, have devised pictorial and figural, nonverbal, or at least partially nonverbal, tests and games for identifying the creatively gifted. Best known of these new tests are the Torrance Tests of Creative Thinking, published by Personnel Press, Princeton, New Jersey. A San Diego elementary school teacher who had been trying Al Hatch's picture tests in disadvantaged areas, says this kind of test is great fun to give—and to take. Also, it has psychological values for the child over and above the identification procedure.

Questions like "What is creativity?" and "How can it be developed?" would require not only a separate chapter but another book to answer. Examples of creatively gifted children and samples of their work (art, writing, ideas) would fill an encyclopedia. Regretfully, I must limit myself to a final recommendation for the identification of creative children so that they may benefit from any special programs that their school system offers for the gifted.

Since, as at least some authorities agree, a good deal of the mental ability that "intelligence tests test" is required for most creative thinking and any *useful* creative production; since that is, creative ability and intelligence do at least overlap—why not lower the required cutoff score on IQ tests for children who demonstrate unusual creativity? (Then maybe that little girl with the IQ of 128 would finally make it!) The tendency to lower cutoff scores has already been remarked by Professor Gowan, and children of above-average mental ability (over 110) who exhibit high creative thinking ability or artistic expression should do well in special programs designed to help them develop their talents. Children of average or below average mental ability might well have difficulty in keeping up with the extra work such programs encourage, although there will always be exceptions.

The lower cutoff score for the creative would also allow some leeway for the culturally disadvantaged child who may have a higher IQ than he can demonstrate on a "white middle-class standardized" intelligence test. On the other hand, children who did not demonstrate any special creative ability or productive talent would probably not be happy in gifted programs unless they demonstrated superior intellectual ability by registering higher scores on the Stanford-Binet.

Unfortunately, the primary complaint in most school systems is that they can't afford to educate all the gifted they've already got, let alone go around looking for any more of them!

The 1971 Report to Congress, based on extensive investigation by a federal task force from the Office of Education, with the cooperation of outstanding educators in the gifted field in many states, disclosed a "nationwide neglect of the gifted." The Congress itself, under the leadership of Senator Jacob Javits (R., N.Y.) and Representative John Erlenborn (R., Ill.), asked for the report in 1969, and the recommendations for doing something about this neglect.

The Report to Congress revealed that almost half of the states have no state personnel in charge of gifted youth education; that only seventeen states and Puerto Rico have full-time Department of Education personnel; and that even where provisions are made, only a handful of the states have made more than a token effort. This was the survey that disclosed that 57 percent of the nation's principals reported *no* gifted children in their school! Yet the most conservative estimate is that 3 percent — 3 in 100 — of the total school population is gifted (for a total of 1.5 million children); many estimates are much higher.

Since the 1971 Report to Congress, some effort has been made to remedy the publicized neglect. The U. S. Office of Education now includes an Office of Gifted and Talented, headed at its inception by Dr. Harold C. Lyon. Currently, Dr. Dorothy Sisk serves as its director. State programs continue to vary in their focus on the gifted; with the impetus from the federal government, a number of them have now joined the pioneers in gifted education — California, Connecticut, Florida, Illinois, Georgia, and New Jersey—in making a commitment to the gifted students in their states. By and large, the classification of gifted children is limited to the academic domain, though the inclusion of talented children is a part of some state programs. Definitions of academic giftedness are clear; criteria for the talented are less well-established and rely—perhaps too heavily—on judgmental factors.

There continues to be, however, even in those areas where resources—money and people—are available, two major problems. First, in order to educate any of the gifted more nearly up to their potential ability to learn, opposition from the community must be overcome—and this is true of almost every community. Too often active opposition or apathy, or a misunderstanding of the nature and needs of bright children are also found among boards of education, superintendents, principals, and teachers—even among *gifted* teaching and administrative personnel!

"I believe they should all stay in high school until they are eighteen," a counselor of 250 gifted students told me the other day, although most authorities agree that some acceleration is advisable for boys and girls who plan to go on to graduate studies. (It's a good idea to get an M.D. or Ph.D. *before* starting a family, but mentally superior boys and girls fall in love just as soon as everyone else.)

Other advisors of gifted students make much of their "emotional problems" even though studies for many years have shown that the gifted generally have fewer, rather than more, emotional problems than the average student. The highly gifted seem to have more difficulties than the moderately gifted; this is often due to boredom in schools that give them no chance to use their remarkable brains.

The second major problem is that in order to educate *more* gifted students schools need more money: for teachers for smaller classes, psychologists for identification, books and other educational materials, field trips, and further pilot programs to find out the best ways to do what has never been done before. My psychology professor used to tell us that psychology was a science in rompers; programs for the gifted are still in diapers. But there are some exciting things happening here and there, and an additional need for money that the Report to Congress uncovered lies in the dissemination of these ideas. That is my major purpose in writing this book, as well as my earlier

Creative Teaching, concerning innovative programs in elementary schools. I am a self-constituted public relations person for better education.

Recently, I suggested to a member of the local board of education that money spent on programs designed for the acceleration of our more able pupils would be more than replaced by the money saved by their getting through school in fewer years.

"We wouldn't want to do that to them just to save money," he replied in horror.

"We'd be doing it to help them," I persisted. "The money we saved would be incidental."

In any case, the two major problems form a circle that one hopes won't be a vicious one. *The more money we can get, the more children we can identify as gifted*, always remembering that far less is or is likely to be spent on the gifted than on the physically or mentally handicapped. In turn, the higher percentage of population we can help by special education for the gifted, the less opposition there will be from the community, and the more support and approval they will give.

The ideal situation would be that all children who wanted the extra learning would be given the chance to participate (self-identification); those who don't want it would be more likely to call it extra work. More and more tests that do not emphasize the intellect are being devised, such as the Torrance Tests of Creative Thinking and Al Hatch's HISC (see "Identifying Potential Giftedness," by Mary Meeker in the National Association of Secondary School Principals *Bulletin*, December 1971). Frank Williams of the University of Oregon and Joe Khatena of Marshall University, Huntington, West Virginia, are making significant contributions to the identification of creative talent. Such tests should be used to supplement mental tests, of course, not replace them.

Site identification is often used to involve more children from deprived communities; teachers who have had the opportunity to observe the children over a period of time know if they have talents or unusual ability in a specific field. Fred L. Strodtbeck of the University of Chicago believes that deprived children often have math and verbal skills, and that Negro girls especially could be trained for math careers. One of the many kinds of special education for outstanding boys and girls is on-the-job training (while still in school) for professional, scientific, technical, business, and other careers that would be of benefit to both individual and society.

Perhaps we are only getting around to the inescapable conclusion that all children are gifted, and that in order to develop the particular gifts of each one, we have to make some long overdue changes in our artificial mass methods of education. These changes are already in operation; pilot schools and classes all over the country are demonstrating the value and practicality of individualized learning, which is the key to freedom.

We must break the molds we have been pouring children into and let each child learn in his own way and at his own pace, as he did so successfully when he learned to walk and to talk. This is the only way we will ever be able to "identify" *all* the gifted and help them learn all they can learn.

SPECIAL INTEREST REFERENCES:

Books and articles that deal with general discussions of giftedness are not nearly as interesting as are case studies about real children. The following are particularly interesting and fascinating to read.

Leta S. Hollingworth. *Children Above 180 IQ.* New York: World Book Co., 1942. This book is out of print, but is available in most college libraries and many city libraries. It is a bit statistical and tedious to read, but one is rewarded at the conclusion by deeper insights into the behavior of some highly gifted children.

Maurice, Freehill, and Hauck, Barbara. *The Gifted: Case Studies.* Dubuque, Iowa: Wm. C. Brown, 1972. Each cash study was contributed by a different educator and requires a focus on individual differences among the gifted as well as differences between groups of gifted. A very important factor in this book is the insightful and functional editorial comments and questions presented by Hauck and Freehill.

2
Intelligence—Born or Bred?
How Important Are Your Parents?

Issues:

How much can environment change a child's potential for high achievement?

Should we "give up" on some children?"

What hope of outstanding achievement is there for the child of average parents?

Why do gifted children and mentally handicapped children sometimes occur in the same family?

At what point should educators feel that a child has achieved his highest possible level of performance?

SIR FRANCIS GALTON (1869): *Where the allowance granted by nature is inadequate, the keenest will and the stoutest industry will strive in vain.*

LEWIS TERMAN AND MELITA ODEN (1947): *That superior achievement tends to run in families has been noted by all students of genius.*

GENE R. HAWES (in a book on testing, 1964): *To this day the question has not been answered in favor of either "nature" or "nurture" as the prime source of intelligence. The best answer seems to be "both" in unknown proportions.*

ARTHUR JENSEN (1969): . . . *we see that the correlation between identical or monozygotic (MZ) twins reared apart is .75.* [See Figure

6, page 50 and other Tables in his *Harvard Educational Review* article for illustrations of his estimates.] *Since MZ twins develop from a single fertilized ovum and thus have exactly the same genes, any difference between the twins must be due to nongenetic factors. And if they are reared apart in uncorrelated environments, the difference between a perfect correlation (1.00) and the obtained correlation (.75) gives an estimate of the proportion of the variance in IQs attributable to environmental differences: 1.00 - 0.75 = 0.25. Thus 75 percent of the variance can be said to be due to genetic variation. . . and 25 percent to environmental variation. Now let us go to the opposite extreme and look at unrelated children reared together. They have no genetic inheritance in common, but they are reared in a common environment. Therefore the correlation between such children will reflect the environment. . . . the proportion of IQ variance due to environment is .24; and the remainder, 1.00 - .24 = .76 is due to heritability.* [His final estimate including all kinship correlations is .81, the widely quoted "80%" inherited.]

CHARLES B. SILBERMAN (1970): *. . . Jensen's argument that black-white differences are largely genetic in origin simply does not stand. As Jencks points out* [Christopher Jencks in *The New Republic*, Sept. 13, 1969] *something like one-sixth of the white identical twins reared in separate homes have as large a difference in IQ—15 points or thereabouts—as that between the average white and the average black. The differences between the twins can be due only to environment, since identical twins always have the same genes.*

LEWIS TERMAN AND MELITA ODEN (1947): *The ancestral strains* [*of 1528 children of IQ 135-200 selected for a study of gifted traits*] *stem back to all the European countries, and to China, Japan, the Philippines, Mexico, Black Africa, and Pre-Columbian America. No race or nationality has any monopoly on brains.*

CHRISTOPHER JENCKS (psychologist and writer, 1969): *Jewish children . . . do better on IQ tests than Christians at the same socioeconomic level, but very few people conclude that Jews are genetically superior to Christians.*

CHARLES SILBERMAN (1970): *Given the present state of knowledge among geneticists, biologists, psychologists, and anthropologists, we simply do not know whether blacks and whites have different gene pools with respect to IQ—nor do we know whether such differences, if they exist, favor one group or the other. Indeed, given the social and cultural environment with which black Americans have had to contend, it is quite possible that they are genetically superior to whites.*

PHILIP VERNON (In *Psychology and Education of Gifted Children,* 1977): *We realize that it (nature of intelligence and its development) varies quite considerably during childhood growth, and is greatly dependent on environmental influences, though this does not mean that we can readily increase the IQ at will. At the same time there is a strong hereditary component both in general and more specialized, abilities.*

LETA HOLLINGWORTH (psychometrist and writer, 1942): *Dixon and Hirsh offer the hypothesis that racial mixture is an antecedent of genius.*

GEORGE I. THOMAS AND JOSEPH CRESCEMBENI *(professors and writers on education for the gifted, 1966): Although a much higher number of gifted children can be identified on the basis of family . . . and cultural background, teachers should not make the assumption that bright children will not be found coming from poor homes or from families where one or both parents have little if any education.*

AUDREY GROST (mother of a genius—1970): *Our progressive educators are as appalled with the expected population explosion of genius intelligence in these [concentrated scientific] communities as they are with the waste in the ghetto.*

JAMES MCPARTLAND (in *The Johns Hopkins Magazine,* April 1970): *Studies have been conducted in the past few years by researchers at Johns Hopkins using the data . . . collected for the Coleman Report on equality of educational opportunity . . . .The Johns Hopkins studies showed that the difference in achievement between the average Negro in a segregated classroom and his counterpart in a mostly white classroom is on the order of one-half standard deviation . . .[i.e.] desegregation serves to cut the racial achievement gap in half. The longer the Negro student spends in a desegregated situation, the more dramatic the improvement in achievement.*

At this point one may add a few recent quotes on school busing, pro and con. This is one of the bitterest controversies of our times, but this debate does at least seem preferable to the situation that existed in not wholly distant times, when buses were segregated.

Peace.

Closely akin to the dispute over "Is special education for the gifted undemocratic?" is the dispute about heredity versus environment in the creation and/or development of a child's mind. Commonly known as the "nature-nurture controversy," this dispute has been going on for many years. Its famous forerunner, Sir Francis Galton's *Hereditary Genius, An Inquiry into Its Laws and Consequences*, was published in 1869, and is available in a World Book Publishing Company edition, 1962.

In the past few years much fiery discussion has centered around the theories of William B. Shockley, Arthur Jensen, and others. These theories not only set forth the conclusion that intelligence is largely hereditary (the figure is often stated as 80 percent) but extrapolates from this premise that an entire race might be inferior in intelligence to another. In certain studies blacks, on the average, scored about fifteen points lower than Caucasians, but this can reasonably be attributed to the typically different environment of the past century and more. This often inferior environment includes factors ranging from poor nutrition to the different cultural background forced upon black people by discrimination in housing, educational facilities, employment, and other vital concerns.

The Supreme Court's 1954 decision, the Freedom March to the Lincoln Memorial, Dr. King's great "I have a dream" speech of 1963, and the championship of the black cause by the younger generation of today effected the beginning of a reversal of this undemocratic policy we have all lived with for so long. (Funny, people never said having special schools for the blacks was undemocratic.) But now anyone, like psychology professor Herrnstein of Harvard, who concludes that intelligence is largely influenced by genetic factors is apt to be called a racist, whether he is or not. Professor Herrnstein's *Atlantic* article, "IQ," said nothing about the intelligence of any race, but merely confirmed Jensen's estimate that intelligence is largely (80 percent) hereditary. Nevertheless he was subjected to personal abuse and threatened with disruption of his classes, whereupon

109 Harvard and Radcliffe professors issued a statement in his defense — the battle *is* bitter!

Far too many words have been wasted on this controversy already. No knowledgeable person disputes that there are many individuals of extremely high intelligence and genius among black people both in Africa and in the United States, in history and on the contemporary scene. Christopher Jencks recently made case records of 12 black children with Binet IQs between 170 and 200; 180 is one in a million. In order to support the premise that blacks are genetically inferior in intelligence to Caucasians, we'd have to come up with the logical conclusion that these blacks must be white! Which is as ridiculous as concluding that white people of low intelligence must be black.

It would be more reasonable to conclude that even granted, as the studies show, that intelligence is 80 percent hereditary and only 20 percent developed or inhibited by environmental factors, we can still explain an average 15 percent of "IQ inferiority" in children whose environments have been inferior. In fact, given the physical, psychological (the "self-image"), social, and cultural advantages that could develop (by 20 percent) the IQ potential of a child (black or white) who lives in a well-to-do professional or business community, and given physical and psychological disadvantages and a different cultural background that could inhibit the development of a child who lives in the ghetto, there could exist a 40 percent spread, allowing for my somewhat creative female logic!

What attention, then, can we give the gifted and talented in all our communities? How can these gifted minds be developed not only to serve our society but to improve it? We can't do anything (yet, anyway) about a child's genes. We can do something about his environment — which includes, above everything except a very good or a very bad home, his education.

Education is in the vanguard of any attempt at permanent improvement of the living environment. Urban renewal projects can raze tenements and substitute new buildings; social welfare projects can improve nutrition and living conditions; a Job Corps can find jobs. But none of these in itself can change or develop the person who lives in that environment, the person who will eventually regress to ghetto life if he does not change. Education should do that. But does it?

It might be best to say what we mean — and do not mean — by

education. We do not mean merely teachers and schools; we mean good teachers and good schools. And we can't exclude, for example, a religious or social worker who in fact teaches the people he or she is trying to help; that's education too, provided it does help, change, develop. Parents, it goes without saying, can be the prime educators, but above all we can no longer underestimate the importance of *the child himself*. Education is not something that is done to a child; it is something he himself accomplishes.

"You know, I learned something from my own thoughts," one child told his teacher in tremendous excitement.

Too many of us have accepted the word education at face value for too long. Anything — including some pretty awful things — that has been offered to us in the name of education we have patiently submitted to since we were five or six years old. And then, after submitting to it for twenty years or so, we — sometimes not so patiently — submitted our children to it.

The children who have suffered most are the gifted, whether they arc the gifted on top of the hill or the gifted in the ghetto. When it comes to this important part of a child's environment — the school he goes to every day until he becomes an adult — both of these children have been deprived, and still are being deprived, of the opportunity to learn anywhere near as much as they are capable of learning.

Worse than that, the rapidly increasing number of critics of authoritarian, lockstep, rote-memory schooling agree that gifted children not only do not learn as much as they could in such schools, they are actually deprived of learning, held back. One study that supports this thesis has been conducted by the San Diego Unified School District in cooperation with the University of California at San Diego. Results show that gifted high school graduates achieve college marks not significantly different from those of less gifted college students. It would appear they have learned not to learn.

When this happens we may lose not only the benefits of these superior intellects; too often the frustration of such a student leads him to questioning of values — sometimes to the ultimate rejection of good. He may "drop out" of society altogether, or he may attempt to destroy it. Remember, he may be one in a million, but throughout history it has been the ones, not the millions, who have changed the course of events for good or evil.

It is no use to pretend, as so many people do, that such persons do not exist. They do exist — and it is estimated that there are about 1.5 million of them in school in the United States right now. That number includes just the highly gifted that we know about. There are millions more gifted children, identified and unidentified, in every city and town and school in our country. And who would say they are not needed?

Much has been said in schools of education for years about motivation of learning. But in practice, what happens? Grades are given that result in the student being motivated to get a good grade; any learning he does is incidental. Bells ring at automatic intervals. How can any high school student get interested in learning 45 or 50 minutes worth of biology followed by the same amount of French followed by a mad dash back from the swimming pool to a measured segment of algebra?

This is the environment our gifted boys and girls are forced to spend most of their childhood and adolescence in. If they are fortunate enough to have good parents, their lives may be enriched by home and travel experiences but family life is not exactly on the upgrade. For the many parents who do want to help their intellectually deprived children, though, suggestions will be found in Chapter 10.

Most children come to school at five eagerly, full of questions, smart little kids who have already taught themselves — "gifted" or not — how to walk and to talk. This is one reason why I am sure there are many more gifted children than we officially recognize, or perhaps, as its proponents claim, *could* develop through "early childhood education."

School should certainly not be an end to learning. Yet it is said that children go into elementary school as question marks and come out as periods.

I can still remember the disappointed face of my five-year-old son David, when he came home from his first day of school.

"They didn't *teach* me anything," he said.

You might say he expected too much the first day but two years ago when he got his Ph.D. he gave a big sigh of relief and said, "I've hated school ever since I was six."

He was one of the lucky ones — he didn't drop out.

If we could make one improvement in the environment of both advantaged and disadvantaged gifted and talented or creative children, it would be to give them a school that they could not wait to go to every morning, a school where they could find happiness in the pursuit of what their special gifts have fitted them for: learning.

SPECIAL INTEREST REFERENCE

Philip E. Vernon. *Intelligence and Cultural Environment.* Scranton, Pennsylvania: New York: Barnes and Noble, 1972.

Here is a scholarly, but easily read, presentation of "the concept of intelligence," how it is determined genetically and how it is influenced by environmental factors. The data include interesting studies of culturally different groups which illustrate the influence of their culture on their abilities.

3
"Since When Was Genius Found Respectable?"
—E. B. Browning
Aurora Leigh

Issues:
　Is it okay to be different?
　What are the responsibilities of "genius" to society as a whole?
　What are the responsibilities of "genius" to self?
　How can schools educate for contribution to benefit mankind and
　at the same time provide for individual fulfillment?

SENECA (First-century Roman philosopher): *There is no great genius without some touch of madness.*

RUTH STRANG (1960): *Contrary to popular opinion, the number of insane geniuses is relatively small.*

LETA HOLLINGWORTH (psychometrist at hospitals, reformatories and prisons who later specialized in the study of highly gifted children, 1942): . . . *to hear of the tremendous differences between the dullest and most intelligent individual . . . is extremely tedious to the average American listener. This is only too well-known to one who has long tried to interest foundations . . . in the education of gifted children. There is an apparent preference among donors for studying the needs and supporting the welfare of the weak, the vicious and the incompetent, and a negative disregard of the highly intelligent, leaving them to "shift for themselves."*

JOHN STUART MILL (19th-century English philosopher and economist who began to study Greek at age three and mastered Latin, classical literature, logic, political economy, history and mathematics by fourteen): *There is always need of persons . . . to discover new truths, and point out when what were once truths are true no longer . . . there are but few persons whose experiments, if adopted by others, would be likely to be any improvement on established practice. But these few are the salt of the earth.*

GEORGE BERNARD SHAW (1923): *It is not easy for mental giants who neither hate nor intend to injure their fellows to realize that nevertheless their fellows hate mental giants and would like to destroy them* [St. Joan].

LETA HOLLINGWORTH (1942): *. . . there are, of course, a majority who are kindly and understanding and helpful, but it is a melancholy fact that there are also malicious and jealous people who are likely to persecute those who are formally identified as being unusual . . . even their instructors, who have felt the impulse to "take them down a peg."*

JOHN STUART MILL: *I insist . . . emphatically on the importance of genius . . . being well aware that no one will deny it in theory, but knowing also that almost everyone, in reality, is totally indifferent to it.*

JAMES J. GALLAGHER (professor and writer on gifted education, 1959): *. . . there is a general tendency to call anything that is different "unhealthy." The child who is interested in atomic physics rather than baseball is thought to be queer.*

LOUISE BATES AMES (1967): *The very bright child often needs help in being a more normal, well-rounded human being.*

LEWIS TERMAN AND MELITA ODEN (1947): *A battery of seven character tests showed gifted children above average on every one. As compared with unselected children they are less inclined to boast or overstate their knowledge; they are more trustworthy when under temptation to cheat; their reading preferences, character preferences, and social attitudes are more wholesome; and they score higher in emotional stability.*

JAMES J. GALLAGHER (1959): *If anything, gifted children, as a group are more emotionally stable, less tense, and more able to handle personal problems than average-ability children. This does not mean that you will not encounter emotionally disturbed gifted children.*

"This is the first time, this year, in my whole life, I wasn't considered weird for reading Camus, Sartre, Freud and anything. Furthermore others were reading the same things and we could sit around and discuss them."

This student opinion from a special program for the gifted in San Diego, California, is a cogent expression of the need for such programs as well as of the feelings of the gifted student himself. It is included in a dissertation by two of the three young men who worked out the program. The two, Dr. David C. Wright and Dr. David P. Hermanson, tested it and then wrote up an evaluation for their Ph.D.'s from the United States International University's Graduate School of Leadership and Human Behavior, in June, 1969. Dr. Hermanson is now Coordinator of Gifted Programs in the San Diego City Schools, the eighth largest school district in the nation. San Diego can offer more to its over 7,000 identified gifted students than is possible in small districts, of course. But the principle behind their innovative Independent Study Unit — a "school within a school" for a selection of gifted, "homogeneous," students — is still under fierce debate.

It would seem reasonable to listen to the point of view of the gifted themselves, especially those at the high school level where their mental ages have reached or exceeded those of many of the adults who have the say about how those brilliant minds are to be developed. This is not to say that even the most gifted do not have anything to learn, still, from adults. They do, and most of them would not want the responsibilities and tedious jobs that go along with administering their educations.

Still, one of the most important things we have to say in this book is that we should *listen* to gifted youth. They have original ideas that are brushed aside, not even considered, for the solution of some of our greatest contemporary problems. And they have the energy, the time, and the brains to work on those solutions if we'll only let them, instead of wasting the most creative years of their lives by foisting upon them rote-memory of out-of-date facts that they have to learn in order to get into college.

It is not hard to understand, if one thinks about it, why some brilliant students drop out of such schools. But as dropouts society has no use for them at all.

Yet even small children in elementary school can help solve community problems. Robert Oppenheimer, the physicist, says there are small children playing in the street who could solve some of his major problems because they have ways of seeing things that an adult has lost. And the head of a town planning commission in Philadelphia actually used elementary school boys and girls; he got them to study and discuss the plans with their parents and other adults, and to study the community itself. They came up with some of the best solutions!

Neil Postman and Charles Weingartner suggested that high school students could form themselves into teams of ten or twelve with a teacher and a community member to study such problems as traffic control, crime, strikes, race relations, urban blight, drug addiction, garbage disposal or air pollution, with the idea of "inventing authentic solutions." But many of today's students express nothing but scorn for the old "student government" idea; they consider it merely a token delegation of authority meaningless in impact. They feel they are capable of a more realistic use of their ideas and skills.

For instance, San Diego had a serious classroom problem based on a legislative decision (the Field Act) that outlaws as earthquake hazards schools built before 1935. Since San Diegans had been using such schools, they suddenly found it necessary to replace several at once; the taxpayers were already bleeding from constantly rising property levies, and in addition, they *liked* those old schools.

This was just one of the problems the kids discussed for starters. One boy suggested that since large apartment construction is creating a need for new schools in their area, the builders should contribute to the construction of those schools. (This was not an original idea; it had been mentioned in the newspapers.)

"They are contributing park land for recreation," the board member pointed out. "A school might be asking too much."

"What do you think about free schools?" a girl named Kellie asked. "Why couldn't the apartment owners just put up a small building in the park? And have a free school?"

As often happens with creative people, she didn't *say* all that she saw in her own mind, and she had already asked so many questions that the board member laughed and said he'd better give someone else a chance. So that was the end of that teenage solution to one of the major problems in many communities today.

But *I* can see what she had in mind: a small, simple, "open" school building in a park, for the children who live all around it; a sort of "free school" but with the School District behind it; the building paid for by men who could afford to build a great many much larger and more elaborate apartment units. They offer tennis courts, golf courses, playgrounds, and swimming pools—why not an elementary school? And perhaps a "middle school" too? Modern "schools without walls" would be comparatively inexpensive, if built along with the apartments, and could be furnished and staffed by the school district. But nobody listens to kids.

After lunch Kim, Terry, Ada, and some of the others took me to see their special room, which has to be the most *colorful* classroom in the world!

The most dazzling feature was their own individual partitioned-off study desks (carrels) that each student had plastered with gaudily designed wallpaper and other bright decorations. There was a frieze around the ceiling painted by Mike, who was also doing an imaginative mural (with everybody's help in the execution) called "Departure of the Spirits." I could tell already from the beginnings of a splendid, rearing horse that it was going to be a work of art.

"I like to draw animals," Mike said. "I read all the books I can get about them, and watch them at the zoo and anywhere."

An inescapable impression one received was that these kids were proud of each other. Caroline, a serious-minded and sedate black who made wise remarks in very few words, admired Kellie (the girl of many words!) for her unconventional ideas. Someone told me Annie was great in Speech and Drama, and a couple of others told me I must read Maria's poetry. From the sheaf of it they showed me I'd say she was one up on Wordsworth already.

Kim put out a newspaper for the group, and planned to write a book called *The Education Machine*. "I like to think up titles," he said, and showed me a poem he wrote called "Technology's Child."

There was an old bathtub in one corner of the room that the kids used for experiments in marine biology, and another corner was partitioned off by bookshelves into a lounge for reading on a comfortable couch and rocking chair, or for small-group meetings. There were heaps of books, not only on the shelves but all over the room.

The City Gifted Program provided funds for books, some to the students themselves, and the teacher had bought hundreds of paperbacks, which Rex, their friend and T.A., was busy cataloging. Even more important, perhaps, were the two computers he managed to acquire for his kids.

The school was under fire as a racially imbalanced school, dominantly black, but its Independent Study Center, including black, brown, white, and Oriental boys and girls, all chosen for their exceptional mental ability, might well be a model for all schools as far as racial mixture is concerned. And this, their gentle, scholarly teacher believes, is even more important than those computers he wangled for them.

At another I. S. Center, at Clairemont High School, I found a long, narrow room with several seminar-type tables. A variety of activities were going on, some so noisy that other groups had to say "Knock it off, will you?" At one of the tables the District Resource Teacher was showing the new editor of their I. S. newspaper how to do headlines; afterwards he asked me to give an informal seminar on feature article writing to which anybody who wanted to could come.

I recognized an old friend of mine at another table—the French wife of a history professor at San Diego State. She came in weekly to give French lessons, the kids progressing as quickly as they wanted to in the language. An art teacher came in, too, for five hours every Friday for the same purpose: to give individualized instruction at a gifted level.

When the two master teachers were introduced I was told, "The one with the beard is the conservative and the one with short hair is the radical." They both laughed.

The "conservative" teaches Honors English, and still believes in the good old classroom lecture. The scientist, the "radical" on the team, is quietly enthusiastic about the concept of independent inquiry.

"This room is full of undiscovered talent," he told me.

All over the United States, such "independent study" plans differ, as do San Diego's high school centers. The nature of independent study itself, school facilities and personnel, and the needs of unique students require differing plans because this kind of education is new and rare in the public schools. Problems of administration and financing must be solved, and only experience with trial plans can develop the solutions.

At some "schools within schools" it is possible for gifted students to spend the whole day with their master teachers, covering the necessary subject matter for graduation in individually designed and group units, or studying on their own and taking "challenge tests" to prove they have mastered the material. They are given free time at school or elsewhere to "do their own thing," and the enthusiasm engendered by this freedom to follow their interests leads to a great deal more learning than they would get in the traditional class. They demonstrate this by in-depth, scholarly papers, scientific experiments, playwriting and production, filmmaking, and in many other creative ways. Students who don't measure up just don't stay in the program.

At La Jolla's highly regarded center, in an older high school building, the kids have two rooms in addition to a small office for the teachers. One room is a small amphitheater for unit lectures and discussion and, when there are no classes, for talking. The other, with individual desks, is the quiet room.

The Independent Study Center at Crawford High has been both highly praised and criticized for its more conservative approach. The teachers and counselor are outstanding, and a copy of the 1971-72 evaluation of their program was printed by the San Diego City Schools as a valuable appraisal of this type of gifted education.

All of the involved students, parents, administrators and teachers are enthusiastic; the chief problem, of course, is to placate those who are not involved. The hope is that these gifted pioneers will blaze the trail to freedom in education for all students — and teachers.

The Report to Congress states, and I have observed this in my visits to some of the schools, that identification of the gifted is hampered by apathy and even hostility among teachers, administrators, guidance counselors, and psychologists.

"Up to last year we couldn't even mention the word gifted," said an elementary school teacher who had had a "cluster" class for several years. "But I think it's finally getting more respectable."

The elementary cluster class includes gifted children transported from surrounding schools (usually by their parents) at a central school, and includes non-gifted students as well. One of its most appreciated benefits, according to parents, is the opportunity for their children to make friends with other gifted children; this is especially important for the rare "genius-type" kid.

Currently (1978-79), the San Diego City Schools are supporting voluntary busing to cluster schools with special programs, as an alternative to compulsory busing. Administrators like Dr. Hermanson, as well as students who willingly leave "advantaged" areas in order to study with minority groups, have expressed enthusiasm about San Diego's experiment in this difficult field of human relations: school busing. While this is not a gifted program per se, it attracts gifted students and makes provisions for them. Dr. Hermanson feels it is "one of the best things that is happening in San Diego today."

"There is an enormous individual and social cost when talent among the nation's children and youth goes undiscovered and undeveloped," the Report to Congress states, along with overwhelming evidence from all parts of the country that this talent is not being developed.

For instance, there is a great need for multilingual people in order to achieve a closer understanding among nations (and our number one goal of world peace), yet many high schools are offering *less* language than they did forty years ago—before the atom was split!

Why? I met gifted students at the Independent Studies Centers who are fascinated by languages—not just one or two, which is all most students can fit into a traditional high school curriculum, but *all* languages.

I ran into a real "language nut." He takes third-year French, fourth-year German (after winning a national German contest that sent him to Germany last summer), and in Independent Studies he's taking Russian.

I love the surprising answers you get when you ask gifted kids questions. "What's the most interesting thing about language?" I asked Craig.

"Grammar," he said. "And I like to look at all languages, and compare the ways of expressing thoughts in different languages."

And I asked him, "What's your favorite language?"

"English."

And, "Do you plan to be a linguist? Teach?"

"I'd like to see what college has to offer before I decide—maybe something in science," he said, "or I might like anthropology if I knew more about it." Languages are useful, of course, in any field.

On a field trip to the Pt. Loma tide pools with another high school group, I sat on the rocks by the ocean and talked to a boy named Tim. Expecting the unusual by now, I got it.

He likes politics—started campaigning at thirteen—and writes political satire.

"I lined up some speaking engagements for one of the local candidates last year at school," he said, "and he didn't come! But frustrations are a part of politics; that's one thing you have to learn."

He quoted from John C. Calhoun on what is the most important thing in politics: "Get elected."

We laughed. He did not mind talking to a strange adult while a boy and girl called to him "See the narwhal," and he kidded back, "If you've seen one narwhal you've seen 'em all." A girl with a remarkable set of values found a smooth pinkish rock shaped like a heart, but threw it back into the ocean because the Pt. Loma tide pools are a restricted area—you can't take anything away.

"What else do you like?" I asked Tim.

"I taught myself German, on my own, after a little Spanish in the sixth grade, and I had two years of Latin in junior high." He went on to mention Arabic, Italian, Japanese, Greek, Portuguese and Russian—in that order—and "the history of linguistic concepts."

His favorite language is Esperanto! He can speak and write it, thinks it is the most euphonious language, and told me it was invented in 1887 by Dr. Ludovic Zamenhof, a Pole.

"I hadn't heard anything about it since I was in college," I confessed.

"There are ten million in the movement now," he assured me, and before our ten minutes or so of conversation was over I knew he also likes astronomy, hates math (except sidereal) and is not looking forward to college because of the social life.

"Don't you have to have a lot of socializing in politics?" I asked.

"That's the part I don't like," he admitted.

Their teacher, the original science man of the pilot Independent

Studies program at Pt. Loma High, was pointing out and explaining the levels of rock structure that reveal its age, and answering questions about marine life in the tide pools. I got to talking to the other teacher on the team who specializes in the humanities, and I mentioned Tim's reluctance about college social life.

He said, "Tim's come a long way. We found him hidden in remedial classes and the corners of regular rooms." He also told me about another girl who is shy; he says Independent Studies is helping her but so far she is just doing "small things — not big things like Tim, but significant for her." They're relating other things to her interest in art.

What a magnificent classroom they had in the vast, sparkling Pacific on a sunny gold day, two teachers who know their fields well enough to answer the sharp questions of the gifted (or most of them!) and the boys and girls themselves, laughing, sliding down the ancient rocks and peering into the tidepools to learn about life under the sea.

Funds for lab equipment are available for the "school within a school" and the teacher calls it "the beginning of a laboratory for the gifted." Professor Gowan says the schools of the future will consist of laboratories and libraries.

I think the two boys I overheard on the rocks saying, "He's a real philosopher besides a scientist," must have been referring to their teacher.

At another Independent Study Center I talked to a senior named Dick, whose chief interest was another surprise.

"I like education," he said enthusiastically. "I read Jerome Bruner's *Process of Education* when I was a sophomore, and I wanted to get into Independent Studies but they wouldn't take me. They called me an underachiever, so I read 26 books and wrote reports and term papers on education and got into the I.S. program at the end of my junior year."

He likes John Holt's books, and is working on a science project on ESP.

Women's Liberationists will be pleased to hear that two 2-time winners of high school sweepstakes in San Diego Science Fair history were both girls: one was red-haired Tamzon, who was also one of the best actresses I ever had in Drama at the Academy of our Lady of Peace; the other, Maureen, was the oldest of a large family, whose first prizewinning entry at Clairemont High was "A Study of the Developmental Enzyme Patterns of Genetically Obese Mice." She won a trip to the International Science Fair in Kansas City during her junior year in high school. There she won a second place award, and then spent the summer at Jackson Laboratory in Bar Harbor, Maine, on a scholarship from the National Science Foundation.

These are just a handful of the "identified" gifted students in one city. I wish I had room for more. If you want to read a delightful book about one genius, I recommend Audrey Grost's *Genius in Residence*. For interesting details about 400 of the most outstanding men and women of the twentieth century, see Victor and Mildred Goertzel's *Cradles of Eminence*.

What happens to bright children in the numerous schools all over the country that make no provision for their extraordinary eagerness to learn? How can the discussion of such children be "tedious?" It is hard to understand our great national inability, or refusal to appreciate, intellectual achievement. It is also hard to forgive, for it causes a constant strain on the resolution of good students to excel in their work. "Peer" pressure to be "just like everybody else" tempts many junior high and high school boys and girls to hide or minimize their talents; surprisingly, twice as many boys as girls become "underachievers," yet girls are often unwilling to seem smarter than the big thing in their lives at that age—boys! Women's Lib may change that attitude, but it has not yet.

Dr. Joanne Rand Whitmore of Peabody College has done interesting research on gifted underachievers—why they become underachievers and what can be done about it. She has a book on the subject coming out in 1979, to be published by Allyn & Bacon.

"I wonder how many people think we are weird?" one of the I.S. girls asked another at Pt. Loma.

"We *are* weird," she laughed.

But "we" was the word that mattered. Good students need friends who understand them, and enjoy the same things.

Although many studies show gifted students to be, if anything, less emotionally unstable than the general population, they are sensitive human beings, with feelings that can be hurt just like anyone else's. They want to be liked.

Some of them are snobs, but so are many people with average IQs.

Some are black, some are white, some are short, some are tall, some are kind, some are mean, some are graceful, some are awkward, some are tactful, some are outspoken.

The only difference between talented and other individuals lies in the talent itself, and *that* is relative. No matter how good one is at anything — tennis, singing, mathematics, or writing poetry, there is always someone who is better (or will be next year). Even if one gets to be number one champion in the world at one thing, look at all the other championships not even approached.

Considering the attitude of so many people toward the gifted, it's really a wonder more geniuses don't turn to evil pursuits. But this is not what happens. One of their outstanding general characteristics is their high moral standards and concern about social problems, which is fortunate for society.

Albert Schweitzer is the personification of this trait. He said, "Whatever you have received more than others in health, in talents, in ability, in success . . . you must render in return an unusually great sacrifice of your life for other life."

A junior high school girl expressed this feeling in a quarter report for a class that included social service at a nearby school for the handicapped.

"My experiences at Sunshine School have been so numerous, pleasant, and enjoyable, that it is hard to put into words my eagerness of going there each morning. . . . I suppose . . . the most important thing I have learned is that I have found my goal in life — teaching handicapped children. The smallest bit of progresss or eagerness displayed by the children fills me with a wonderful sense of achievement. Little words and actions expressing emotions and feelings are most important to me — a smile, a hug, a greeting, a proud voice saying 'Look what I've made!' . . ."

In the past, gifted children have managed to sit through twelve or thirteen years of monotonous schooling and still become great social, intellectual, scientific, and industrial leaders. But let us see, in Chapter Six, what that type of education is like for the children.

SPECIAL INTEREST REFERENCES:

Grost, Audrey, *Genius in Residence*. Englewood Cliffs, N.J.: Prentice Hall, 1970. Do you want to know how it is to live with a gifted child—at least this one? Read and find out. Here is a delightful book.

Goertzel, Victor and Mildred *Cradles of Eminence*. Boston: Little, Brown and Company, 1962 ". . . an original study of the parentage, education, early environments and childhoods of over 400 men and women of the twentieth century." There are many surprises in this volume and information about the subjects which broadens our understanding. Should be number one on your "must read" list. Look for a forthcoming follow-up, too. It is to be entitled *300 Eminent Personalities*, and will include some more recent outstanding men and women, including Golda Meir, T. S. Eliot, Che Guevara, and Helen Hayes.

4

Is Special Education for the Gifted Undemocratic? What Is "Equal Education?"

Issues:

Must special education for the gifted result in an aristocracy of the intelligent?

How can schools provide for academic needs of students and at the same time develop in them a respect for the worthiness of others?

What will happen to our world if potentials of able persons are not achieved?

Are the gifted as worthy of attention as the handicapped?

MRS. NORMAL: *Why should my taxes be spent for special education for your child?*

MRS. BRIGHT: *Many authorities agree that gifted students can do the work in from one to three years less time. One year's schooling in the U. S. costs about $15 billion. So if my child can get through school faster, that will save taxes.*

MRS. NORMAL: *She can't get through faster. That's undemocratic!*

PLATO (a deep voice from the 4th century B.C., chuckling): *Democracy . . . is a charming form of government, full of variety and disorder, and dispensing a sort of equality to equals and unequals alike.*

THOMAS JEFFERSON: *We must dream of an aristocracy of achievement arising out of a democracy of opportunity.*

JAMES RUSSELL LOWELL: *It was in making education not only common to all, but in some sense compulsory on all, that the destiny of the free republics of America was practically settled.*

SAMUEL BUTLER (19th-century English writer, painter and composer): *I do not think America is a good place in which to be a genius.*

WILLIAM RASPBERRY (columnist for the Washington Post, 1976): . . . *What begins as an attempt to democratize education too often ends in "mediocritizing."*

BERTRAND RUSSELL (English philosopher, 1926): *The American public schools achieve successfully a task never before attempted on a large scale; the task of transforming a heterogeneous selection of mankind into a homogeneous nation.*

JOHN CURTIS GOWAN (professor emeritus, writer, and Executive Director of the National Association for Gifted Children, with George Demos, 1964): *How do we harmonize the opposing principles of developing each individual to his maximum and at the same time provide for the greatest general good through a common education?*

ALFRED GITELSON (Judge, County of Los Angeles Superior Court, Case 822854): *Equal education is the foundation of the right to be a human being. . . . This does not mean that any gifted child or any child having a greater ability to learn may or shall be deprived of his or her opportunity to learn to the best of his or her ability. That opportunity must be made available to all on equal terms.*

JEROME BRUNER (educator and writer, 1960): *One thing seems clear: if all students are helped to the full utilization of their intellectual powers, we will have a better chance of surviving as a democracy in an age of enormous technological and social complexity.*

RUTH STRANG (Professor of Education, 1960): *Democracy requires diversity rather than uniformity. Valuable individual differences need to be cultivated. . . . Few people object to making special provisions for the athlete, or for the handicapped child. Gifted children may become handicapped if appropriate provision is not made for them.*

JOHN W. GARDNER (former President of the Carnegie Corporation and Secretary of Health, Education and Welfare, 1961): *Those who are most deeply devoted to a democratic society must be precisely the ones who insist upon excellence. . . . The idea for which this nation stands will not survive if the highest goal men set for themselves is an amiable mediocrity.*

JOHN HOLT (teacher and writer, 1970): *Human experience, knowledge, culture is everyone's. No one ought to have to prove that he deserves it. It ought to have been used for a great upward leveling, to make a universal aristocracy of wisdom and learning. It was and is used instead to make a hierarchy, a pyramid of men, with the learned men self-placed at the top.*

ELIZABETH DREWS (in the January-February 1976 issue of *Today's Education*): *By some distortion of the notion of equality, attention to the special needs of the gifted has been viewed as elitist or downright undemocratic. And within the ranks of the creative minority itself, the most significant minority of all—those whose excellence is ethical and humanitarian—have been traditionally ignored while scientific and mathematical talent has been encouraged. Yet what use is it to train the mind if the morals are corrupted. A higher than average intelligence linked to a lower than average ethic is a positive menace to society.*

There is something to be said for both positions, as with all the controversial quotations heading our chapters, but recently a new dimension has been added to the discussion that may resolve this conflict. It may not be democratic to devote special attention and state and federal funds to "the gifted" if we continue to find most of these children in wealthy and/or professional families. Studies have consistently shown that the great majority of the "identified gifted" come from "high socioeconomic communities."

We are just beginning to realize, however, that there are children with *undiscovered* talents and leadership qualities (even more in need of development) in our slums and ghettoes, in poor rural communities or in families that are always on the move.

"Give me your tired, your poor, your huddled masses yearning to breathe free" was inscribed on the Statue of Liberty in New York harbor in 1908, yet we have huddled masses yearning to breathe free in all our cities today. In our plans to educate the gifted we must include talented and creative citizens who can't pass the mental-cultural tests we have so long used as the sole criteria for success in school and in life.

If we can find and educate *all* our potential leaders to the limit of their capacities to learn, then we will have a genuine democracy with equal opportunity for leaders from every community.

But from *every* community—we must be careful not to go to an opposite extreme and underrate the vital contributions of the often unjustly resented "élite." They have contributed, and will continue to contribute, much to human knowledge, comfort, and enjoyment of life for everyone: a telescope (Galileo's father was a wealthy merchant), a treatment or cure for a formerly fatal disease, a symphony, or a television set.

Geniuses constitute a minority regardless of what color they are; the number of geniuses is estimated at one-half to one percent of the total population, although the gifted and talented may include from 20 to 30 percent, depending on what criteria are used. New kinds of tests, such as nonverbal tests for creativity, will increase the percentage, and perhaps some genius will devise a way in which we could all become geniuses.

Experiments in this field are already under way (asexual reproduction, DNA, RNA—and how about brain transplants?) I can not say I am in any hurry for this millenium; one of the most fascinating things in creation is our individual differences. But we are going to need all the gifts we have got, and with the spiralling complexity of our society we can use more geniuses than ever before, as well as plenty of good, intelligent, and willing people to carry out their ideas.

A high school counselor says, "The gifted kid is the neglected kid. Gifted kids are turning off all over." And his school is in an "advantaged" district.

We cannot discriminate against a child because his family has money or high social position, no matter how strongly we feel that it is time to help those who have not had such advantages to obtain them. We can not use this as an *excuse* to do nothing for "the rich kids." (Who wants to pass the plate for a Rockefeller, as someone put it!) Oddly enough, it is not so much the poor that take this attitude as it is the equally well-to-do anti-intellectual. And the "rich kids" aren't always rich in money.

In this book we will examine programs and ideas for all the gifted, and we'll discuss new ways of finding them. Federal funds and popular opinion currently favor the children who have been deprived so long because of poverty or prejudice, so this is an especially opportune time to help them, and to foster this spirit so it will be continued long enough to get substantial results.

Justice has a pair of scales that sometimes has to be overloaded on one side in order to compensate for the fact that it was formerly overloaded on the other. The basic democratic sense of fair play among the majority of Americans is finally surfacing, although we live in a period of dissatisfaction for people who feel we are doing too little—or, on the other hand, too much—for racial minorities. A meeting of the minds of our brightest boys and girls from all communities could eventually eliminate the "race problem."

Dr. David Hermanson, District Coordinator of Gifted Programs in the San Diego, California, city schools, has developed, over the years,independent study centers that work toward this ideal, and other interesting programs such as clusters of students identified by IQ criteria. These programs have served as models for programs thoughout California and other parts of the country.

Professor E. Paul Torrance of the University of Georgia, whose name has become a byword for *creativity*, says that in the future we'll have to depend on gifted members of disadvantaged and minority cultures for most of our creative achievements.

A concerned teacher of educationally handicapped children, asks this: "Why do we expect to find the leaders and creative artists of the future among the minority cultures? Because they're hungry. They're hungry for the self-image, the material security, and the upward mobility.

"What does a rich kid want? They grow up with everything. There's no tension, no problems to solve. They seem like they're in a vacuum—they float.

"But the deprived—not all of them, the creative ones—have a deep rage, and a need to express this rage."

Can they do it? Yes, with help, although the creative arts may not be the best path to *material* security. Creative minds are needed in all fields, however, not only in poetry and painting. But the "rich kids" are needed too. Professor Lewis Terman's Stanford follow-up studies of 1,000 gifted California children of the 1920s to mid-life in the 1950s show that 45 percent of the men were in the professions and 26 percent in important semi-professional and business positions. Of the 48 percent full-time employed women, 61 percent were in professions, 35 percent in business. What would we do without such leaders?

Even more important, perhaps, in this age of "enormous technological and social complexity," will be the one in a hundred thousand to one in a million mentally gifted kids — the geniuses. As James B. Conant and others have pointed out, the highly gifted are an entirely different group from the academically talented and should be treated quite differently. But this distinction is seldom made, "the gifted" with IQs of from 120 or so to 200 are usually grouped together in spite of their different needs and potential contributions. The highly gifted child — variously defined, but generally scoring above 145 — is as different from the child in the lower ranges of giftedness (128-138 or so) as is the average from the below average child. The elements that make up this differentness must be sorted out and dealt with by parents and schools. We need the most complex brains as well as the highly creative to sort out the tangle of new knowledge and invention.

Now, when changes are exploding all around us whether we like them or not; when our latest younger generation has expressed frustration and disillusionment to the point of destruction and despair; we need a new generation of creative thinkers and dreamers from all our communities to plan and construct an orderly world of tomorrow.

This new generation has to come from the gifted children of today.

SPECIAL INTEREST REFERENCES:

Gardner, John, *Excellence: Can We Be Equal and Excellent Too?* New York: Harper and Row, 1961. Don't be misled by the "age" of this book; it is timeless. It contributes greatly to the controversy described in this chapter. It is a bit disquieting in its charge, but is a stimulating challenge to all of us who feel some responsibility for the future of the human and his environment.

5
What about Early Childhood?
"Is Sooner Better?"

Issues:
  Should the goal of early education be largely socialization?
  What happens to a child if we push too hard?
  What happens to a child if we don't push hard enough?
  What are those experiences in early childhood which have the greatest utility for a normal, wholesome development of self?

PLATO (about 2400 years ago): *The most important part of education is right training in the nursery. (Laws, 643).*

MARIA MONTESSORI (Italian foundress of the Montessori Method of early childhood education popular in modern advanced preschools, 1917): *Woe to us, when we believe ourselves responsible for matters that do not concern us, and delude ourselves with the idea that we are perfecting things that will perfect themselves quite independently of us. . . . What a relief to say: "Nature will take care of that. I will leave my baby free, and watch him grow in beauty; I will be a quiescent spectator of the miracle."*

MAYA PINES (writer-reporter, under a Carnegie grant, 1966): *Millions of children are being irreparably damaged by our failure to stimulate them intellectually during their crucial years—birth to six.*

FITZHUGH DODSON (psychologist, educator, founder of La Primera Preschool, consultant Head Start, 1970): *. . . the more intellectual stimulation you can give your child in the first five years of his life,*

58

without pushing or pressuring him, *the brighter and more intelligent he will become, the higher IQ he will have as an adult.*

SIEGFRIED AND THERESE ENGELMANN (husband, Institute of Research on Exceptional Children, University of Illinois; wife, degrees in psychology and law, 1966): "The parent is not qualified to educate." *This argument is rapidly becoming obsolete as more and more educators recognize the value of preschool training.*

MARIA MONTESSORI (1914): . . . . *The child has a personality which he is seeking to expand; he has initiative, he chooses his own work, persists in it, changes it according to his inner needs; he does not shirk effort, he rather goes in search of it, and with great joy overcomes obstacles within his capacity. . . . There is therefore no need of intervention. "Wait while observing." That is the motto for the educator.*

BENJAMIN FINE (Headmaster, Sands Point [New York] Academy Country Day School for Gifted Children, journalist and educator, 1965): *In my opinion bright children are ready to enter school at 3½ years of age.*

LOUISE BATES AMES (of the Gesell Institute of Child Development, 1967): *We think [early entrance into kindergarten programs] do harm in that they arrange for the child young in years but bright in mind . . . to be placed in a grade for which his age (and therefore in all probability his behavior level) makes him unready, even though there may be no question of his brightness.*

RUTH MARTINSON (professor whose interest in gifted education has been instrumental in forming State and national policy, in a research summary for the Report to Congress, *Education of the Gifted and Talented*, Vol 2, 1971): *Children who read before the age of school entry, and understand mathematical concepts commonly taught to far older children, . . . also tend to be generally more mature than others of their age. It should not be necessary to retard their development until they attain an arbitrary chronological age required for school entry.*

FITZHUGH DODSON (1970): . . . *disadvantaged children of poor parents actually enter kindergarten or first grade considerably behind in intellectual ability as compared with the children of mid-dle class parents. And the poor children never catch up, due to the lasting effects of the lack of intellectual stimulation in their early years. This is why the Head Start programs attempt to give these children enough intellectual stimulation in their early years so that they will not be hopelessly educationally handicapped throughout their school years.*

CHARLES SILBERMAN (in his 3½-year study of American schools commissioned by the Carnegie Corporation, 1970): . . . *the results of Head Start and other preschool programs [are] disappointing—initial gains seem to wash out by the second or third grade.*

EDUCATIONAL POLICIES COMMISSION, NATIONAL EDUCATION ASSOCIATION (May 1966): *All children should have the opportunity to go to school at public expense beginning at the age of four.*

Here the poor parents find themselves beleaguered by two opposing armies of experts. I used to think doctors were infallible until one told me my first son *must* be circumcised, and another said, "Do you want to mutilate him?"

I had to choose.

Pros and cons on early childhood education both make sense, however, so perhaps this choice is not a matter of life or death, either.

The kind and amount of preschool education is one of the earliest and most important decisions parents have to make in raising a child. Oddly enough, considering parental inexperience at this point, studies have shown that gifted children are more often first or only children, although, of course, some geniuses do come along a lot later. Ben Franklin was the fifteenth in his family!

Mothers are able to devote their undivided attention to a first baby, of course; this would substantiate the findings of a growing number of researchers who are concluding that human beings never learn as rapidly as they do before the age of three, and that if we start educating them in infancy we can actually affect their future IQ scores.

Ever since Alfred Binet, at the beginning of this century, devised a way to measure intelligence, most children's scores have remained fairly constant, varying by no more than ten to fifteen points throughout the school career. A child was considered average, below average, or retarded; or above average, superior, or highly gifted. Now, psychologists and child development specialists tell us parents may be able to convert children who would otherwise grow up to be of average intelligence into gifted children simply by talking to them and providing them with many different experiences while they are still in their bassinets.

Children's centers all over the country are teaching and testing "tiny tots" during these crucial years in the development of intelligence. And no less an authority than the Harvard Graduate School of Education admits that the mother is the "single most important environmental factor." (Isn't that a switch?) It has been stated frequently that 80 percent of a child's intelligence is determined *before* birth, but some dramatic changes in small children's IQs (including gains of as much as 30 points) have been effected by more intensive education (by mothers or in the centers) than the average baby gets. Few people ever thought six- to fifteen-month-old babies *could* learn much.

On the other hand, these studies are so new that important follow-up tests are still lacking. It isn't after all so surprising that a child who has been "tutored" (as in the National Institute of Mental Health's "intelligence boosting" project under Dr. Earl Schaefer) averaged 17 points higher on IQ tests than a random sampling of three-year-olds in the same neighborhood who hadn't been taught for an hour every day for 21 months. How will these same children compare in five or ten years? In college? No doubt such follow-ups will be made, and it seems quite possible that there will be some permanent gains. I doubt if all the mothers who knock themselves out trying will turn out many more geniuses than we usually have, but it would be great if they could.

We can use all the gifted kids we can get in our increasingly complex society. Outstanding characteristics of exceptionally intelligent children are that they can work with abstract ideas, see relationships, and understand new concepts. Obviously, these gifts will be needed more than they ever have been in the much simpler past. Increased knowledge requires greater ability to perceive relationships and effects of knowledge on human behavior. We have the knowledge to destroy bugs, forests, and people; we have the knowledge to solve the problems of pollution, poverty, and energy (though we don't use it); we know how to get to, and travel on, the moon. The wisdom with which we use and evaluate what we know in human terms will determine the manner in which man continues to survive.

As will become apparent throughout this book, I believe that compromise can usually be effected between two extreme views, and that such a middle course will generally be the wisest. We need people like Maria Montessori to say "let them be" and others like the revolutionary Maya Pines to say that millions of them will be irreparably damaged if we do let them be, in order to test out those theories and find the happy medium — the golden mean.

The inspiration for an article for *Parents Magazine*, which expresses my own feelings about early childhood education, was our youngest son, Johnny; he was gifted but, like most parents, we had not yet learned of this when he was four. I thought then, and still do, that all children are more original and imaginative before they go to school and start reading books and writing clichés.

The article is reprinted here, in part.

The Wonderful Age of Four

A four-year-old is somebody special. Not quite a baby and not quite a real little boy or girl, not quite a cherub and not quite an imp, his innocence is wondrous and his wisdom appalling!

At four he can take time out to rest from the stupendous tasks every infant has to face: he has learned to walk and to talk and to act rather like other people.

In another year or so he will have to start his education and learn how to read and write and sit still in school. But nobody expects anything of him now; he doesn't even have to grow much this year — he has time. But he does have to find out about things.

That's why he asks so many questions. When he was two or three, he was just as curious, but what he wanted to know was how things feel and smell and taste; that's why he got into everything.

At four, he doesn't always need to touch all that he wonders about and his researches soar into the realm of philosophy. From somewhere, he has picked up a vocabulary that constantly amazes his parents. Use a word once in his hearing and it's his. Some evening when you tell him it's time to go to bed he will confound you by announcing, in grown-up language, "I prefer to stay up." And from this day forward your confidence in your omnipotence as a mother will be shaken: sometimes you will even doubt the truth of that comforting adage: "Mother knows best." Maybe you don't!

He will certainly inquire about the universe and who made it, where he comes from and where he is going—the idea of God is easy for him to grasp and heaven becomes, with no difficulty, the synonym for whatever makes him most happy. He does not have to see to believe. . . .

His thinking is original, not cluttered with clichés the rest of us have acquired. If you listen you will find out that often he talks in poetry.

"What do you do when you go to sleep?" someone asks him.
"I dream."

"And what do you do when you wake up?"
"Turn the sunshine on!"

Stars fascinate him and he loves to wish on them. What joy when, after making a wish, he shouts, "Daddy, Daddy, that star I wished on twinkled!"

He observes, "Thunder makes a lot of noise. Lightning is not loud, but it makes the windows pretty." . . .

His logic will confound the most brilliant of scholars and woe be unto the relative who tries to tease a four-year-old. The psychologist, giving him an intelligence test, frequently gets an answer he didn't expect, though indubitably correct. "Repeat, 'I have a little dog,'" says the tester and back comes the unanswerable "I haven't. . . ."

Sometimes you may suspect that he has no sense of humor; but don't you believe it. When his grandmother asks him how old he is, he says, "I am four, and how old are you?" . . . He will spend hours playing that his rocking horse is a car and the vacuum cleaner a filling station ("SSSSS! Fill'er up!") but if you join in his pretending and suggest that a picture of a car in a magazine is real enough to ride in, he will inform you with the utmost condescension, "You can't get in it. It's just a picture." What does he believe and what doesn't he? You never know. . . .

Read him a story. He likes, he will tell you, stories about "boys and girls a-playing and a-living and a-swinging and a-do-ing." But put his name in , make him the hero of them all, because at four he sees everything with himself in the middle.

"What is a book?" you ask him.
"They're to read me a story."

"And what is a blanket?"
"A blanket is to get me snug and warm."

"What is a street?"
"A street is to keep out of so I won't get my bones all broken up."

"What is a fence?"
"To make babies stay in. . . ."

Ask any four-year-old such questions and you will get a pretty good idea of his parents, his environment, his character and anything else you want to know.

Last year you were so busy washing his pants and keeping him out of mischief that you didn't have much time left over just to talk with him and to play with him. Next year he will go to school and someone else will tell him the answers, or he will read them in a book.

But this year is yours; and your cherub, your imp, your little boy or girl belongs all day long and every day to you. It is a time of innocence, of wisdom and of wonder.

Parents' Magazine
December 1958

As may be apparent from this article I didn't believe that four-year-olds should be packed off to the rat race of school; four seemed a good year to rest after the tremendous accomplishments of learning to walk and talk that, interestingly most children seem to do almost equally well in about the same period of time and without teachers. Also, for many years parents (generally) have done a good job during the important "first six years," which many psychologists have agreed is "when a child's character is largely formed." American parents would be very much against the state taking over this function (character formation).

But there is the question, "What about children whose parents are not so good, or have to work?"

With more and more mothers working, especially in poorer homes where it takes two salaries to contend with the inflation (or where there is no father), day-care centers are essential, and Women's Liberationists are demanding them for wealthier career-mothers as well.

Pre-schools and nursery schools are in abundance throughout the country today. (A "walk through the yellow pages" under schools will confirm this.) Day-care centers, which range from educational to custodial, have been standard fare for many years; our children all went for one year to the college Home Economics nursery school when they were three. Its chief value was social.

Where there are good parents, with mothers at home and playmates available but no affordable nursery school nearby, it is certainly a good idea to form groups of mothers who can share the care *and* do a little educating too. In view of the latest research findings on the pre-school intellect, we had better do just that. A rested mother can read to a group of children, teach them to paint or dance or speak a language — whatever each mother has to contribute — and it's all free. If you want to do this on a more ambitious scale, *Day Care: How to Plan, Develop and Operate a Day Care Center* is helpful. (See Bibliography)

Early childhood education in public schools has been tried over the last decade. In the early 1970s San Diego established multi-age classrooms for children aged four to six. Palo Alto has organized and maintained an Adult Education Pre-school program that provides experiences once a week for two-and-a-half year olds; a twice-a-week program for three-year-olds and a three-times-a-week program for four-year-olds. Parents make a commitment to help with classroom activities on a regular basis and return afternoons or evenings to participate in discussion groups. California's forward-looking Early Childhood Education (ECE) bill included additional state monies for extra efforts, on the behalf of younger children, by school districts that included the four-year-olds in ECE. When the bill became law in the fall of 1973, the four-year-old aspect of it had been eliminated — presumably through the pressure of the nursery school lobby. State Superintendent Dr. Wilson Riles's heart was in the right place, but politically it didn't fly.

Authorities recognize the need for preschool classes for the physically handicapped or mentally retarded, who need a longer time to prepare for first grade. This is also true for children with diverse cultural backgrounds, some of whom never even hear English spoken in their homes.

Advanced school districts provide special schools, classes, or tutors for different types of handicaps; these classes are usually state or federal financed. Head Start is the well-known federally funded kindergarten-prep for the "disadvantaged." An admirable feature of Head Start is the involvement of parents as well as children; mothers are expected to help with the program. The chief criticism has been that the gains children initially make may be wiped out several years later, in elementary school. The Follow Through program was designed to prevent the loss of gains made by children in the Head Start program. Evaluations are currently being conducted to determine the degree to which it has been successful in this effort.

Is earlier better? If we are simply going to add a "grade" or two before kindergarten that is similar to the grades we already have — NO. (Kids have to waste enough of the sunshine hours of their childhood as it is.) If we're going to coop them up in a room all day, or even half a day, and *direct* their learning instead of leaving them free to find things out for themselves—NO. However, if small children were free to learn, each at his own pace, and to teach each other, in individualized, ungraded classes where a rich choice of activities is provided along with plenty of teachers and teacher-aides to help and guide them, starting earlier would be beneficial to many children—especially to gifted and talented boys and girls who have no such opportunities at home.

Children under five are unquestionably able to learn much more than they do. Gifted children (some authorities believe average children too) can read and are probably more ready at two or three than when they are held back until age six. One little girl read the labels on her baby-food cans at two and then lost interest when her parents, fearing that she shouldn't learn to read so soon, let the opportunity pass. She has never been much interested in reading since, although she is now in the seventh grade—an "underachiever" with a high IQ. Compare her to the small boy who is happily reading at third-grade level in "independent study" in one of the experimental four- to six-year old classrooms. He is four.

Disregarding the geniuses of the past who could read Greek or play concertos at three, there are many children in our own times who have learned to read at that age. You can teach your own child to read, or let him teach himself. Preferably, provide him the opportunity to teach himself.

When a bright child is ready to read, it is hard to stop him. A parent's greatest contribution at that time can be to provide opportunities for him to develop his reading vocabulary. Linger longer in the market, drive slowly by road signs. Basically, provide a rich word environment and get out of the way. Our intuitive reader—and that's what most bright chidren are—needs to set his own pace and will need little instruction. Such instruction should consist of short, simple answers to questions. If he wants to know more about penguins than you have told him, he'll ask. The verbally precocious preschooler who has to be taught to read should not be taught to read. Parents can do more for him by providing him with a great variety of experiences so that when he is ready to "take off" his repertoire of concepts is as vast as possible. He easily learns the word *bird* when he can visualize a bird; he learns the words *park, market, ship,* when he can visualize them.

Early reading is the most prevalent distinguishing trait of gifted children. But remember, one does not read only words—one reads clouds, trees, people, the wind, street cars. Calling words is not reading—understanding is reading.

But, if your child does show early signs of being gifted and you want to help him, or her, develop those gifts, you'll have to resign yourself to some criticism even though, in this generation, you can also find some support. Audrey Grost's *Genius in Residence,* which recounts her son Mike's early childhood years and what the neighbors said, is one of the most entertaining books a mother with the same problems could read. It's *never* easy. The story of Friedrich Froebel, who founded the first kindergartens in Germany in 1836, sounds like that of a revolutionary educator today. He too believed that education should begin at birth, that teachers and parents should allow children to follow the lines of their own interest, that *planned* play and games can teach as well as amuse. And he too was fiercely opposed; in 1851 a law was passed forbidding the establishment of kindergartens!

Maria Montessori is more popular today than ever, although she developed her ideas about the education of preschool children in 1906 in Italy, and they soon became popular in other countries, too. She believed it important to develop the child's senses in the years from one-and-a-half to five, and, as in the English nursery and infant schools, she used plenty of concrete materials, including her famous "Children's House." The important consideration was *self-education*; the children were in charge of the house, objects in it were breakable, and the children were not told "Don't touch!"

They learned because things broke.

The giant figure in educational psychology today is Jean Piaget; he has probably had more influence on educators than any thinker since John Dewey. And he formed his ideas on early childhood education, as all parents should, *on his own children,* and others with whom he shot marbles while asking questions.

Mothers and fathers who spend time with their children every day, talking to them, reading with them, playing games, listening to music or a good TV show, taking walks, camping, or visiting museums, can teach their small ones more than they would learn in a school. Many years ago my husband took our oldest daughter, then four, to an opera.

"What was that opera you took Frea to?" I asked him recently.

When he didn't remember, I called her up (she has children of her own now). "Oh, it was Carmen," she said. "That was so much fun."

I remember Johnny in his bassinet at five weeks refusing to go to sleep to anything but *classical* records; Daddy reading a rumbly Pooh and a squeaky Piglet, and playing the piano for us all to sing out of *The Fireside Book of Folk-Songs*.

We discussed history and geography on trips in our old Packard: once we were driving through the Southern states and talking about the Civil War. Our second daughter, Sheila Mary, then about nine, read a sign on a store.

"Who was General Merchandise?" she asked.

Serious discussions with our philosophical four-year-olds:

"How was I started?"

"What does God stand on?"

"If everybody in the world was good, we wouldn't need any policemen, would we?"

For the children of parents who can't (or won't) provide that kind of early childhood education, we do need schools. But not just as an extension of the long, dull years from "K through 12." Children, especially the gifted, should be allowed to learn as much as they want to, as fast as they want to — and as soon as they want to.

That's the only way they ever *will* want to.

SPECIAL INTEREST REFERENCES:

Fraiberg, Selma, *Magic Years*. New York: Scribner, 1968. Focuses on the special qualities of young children and on the need to look at the total development of a child — not just the intellectual aspects of his or her growth.

Briggs, Dorothy, *Your Child's Self-Esteem*. New York: Doubleday, 1975. Self-esteem is an essential characteristic in all youngsters. This "handbook" for families of pre-school children includes general guidelines for the early years as well as discussions of exceptionalities in children.

Kindergarteners in Pat Robinson's class in Palo Alto, California, write journals daily; they choose a word, write it, read it, illustrate it, and then dictate a story about it. In the photo a youngster dictates his "mouse story" to Ruthe Lundy, Coordinator of programs for the gifted in Palo Alto. (Photo courtesy of Pat Robinson)

Early reading is the most prevalent trait of gifted children. When they are ready to read, you cannot stop them! (Photo courtesy of San Diego Unified School District)

6
Are Bright Children Bored in Our Schools?
"Do I Hafta Go to School Today?"

Issues:

Are schools meeting the needs of gifted students?
Are there alternative ways to teach gifted students?
How can the conflict between "covering the material" and responding to students' interests be resolved?
What part does motivation play in teaching students of all abilities?
How do motivational techniques differ for the gifted?

MARIA MONTESSORI (1912): . . *in* . . . *public schools* . . . *the children are repressed in the spontaneous expression of their personality till they are almost like dead beings. In such a school the children, like butterflies mounted on pins, are fastened each to his place, the desk, spreading the useless wings of barren and meaningless knowledge which they have acquired.*

ALBERT EINSTEIN (quoted in *Einstein*, ed. Paul Schlipp, 1951): *It is in fact nothing short of a miracle that the modern methods of instruction have not yet entirely strangled the holy curiosity of inquiry.*

SENATOR JACOB JAVITS (in the *Congressional Record*, Jan. 28, 1969): *The talented child has often been the forgotten child and the underachiever despite his extraordinary potential because he becomes bored with unchallenging programs.*

LOUISE BATES AMES (1967): *The bright child is seldom bored in school.*

JOHN HOLT (1970): *Almost all children are bored in school. Why shouldn't they be? We would be.*

JAMES BRYANT CONANT (1959): *In all but a few of the schools I have visited* [he personally visited one-half of over 100 high schools in 26 states for this study] *the majority of the bright boys and girls were not working hard enough.*

WILLIAM RASPBERRY (Public Affairs columnist for the *Washington Post*): *The most neglected and universally denigrated group in every big city high school is the mentally gifted.*

HERBERT KOHL (teacher and writer, 1967): *How can the children be expected to be alert, curious, and excited when the teacher is so often bored?*

ALVIN I. EURICH (educator and writer on educational reform, 1969): *Many behavior problems disappear when children are challenged intellectually.*

MARK VAN DOREN (poet and professor): *Freedom to use the mind is the greatest happiness.*

GEORGE LEONARD (journalist, 1968): *Education, at best, is ecstatic.*

ELIZABETH DREWS (teacher and writer, 1972): *The creative and gifted students reach out beyond the amassing and recall of facts.*

"Well, now, take my courses as an example, I've had the courses in junior high school. We read one chapter a week, complete one work sheet a week, and have a movie on Friday. The instructor is so lazy that I run the projector and we even exchange tests for correction which are true-false types. It's a bore, waste of time, but if I don't play the game I won't get into college."

This high school student's opinion, taped in 1968 for the Hermanson and Wright dissertation, contrasts sharply with that of the boy who started off so eagerly, "This is the first time, in my whole life, I wasn't considered weird for reading Camus, Sartre, Freud. . . ."

The problem of boredom is especially critical for the highly gifted. Champions of education for the gifted rarely make any distinction, but when possible we should. (There is as much difference between 135 and 170 as there is between 100 and 135.) Studies have shown that, among the total gifted population, emotional and behavioral problems are no more common or indeed less common than in the general population. Among the few with extremely high IQs, however, there may be more cases of maladjustment, and this is not surprising.

In a high school honors math class, my daughter sat next to a boy who never did any homework and composed music in his notebook while the rest of the class tackled the difficult problems that their teacher liked to bring in for them. "Sometimes," Frea said, "when we all got stuck, including the teacher, Tom would look up and straighten us out."

This boy got a C in math, along with poor grades in other subjects, because he didn't do the work; with that scholastic average he didn't go to college. "I don't think he even wanted to," Frea said. "He was a nice-looking, normal type of boy but he never had any friends or participated in anything but the band for a while. He never made any trouble; he just didn't care."

When the Bank of America awards were given to the seniors, Frea was as surprised as we were when she got the one in math.

"A boy like Tom ought to get that," she said.

We wonder what happened to him, and are curious to see whether he may still use that fantastic mathematical ability. How many of the few who have it become Einsteins and Norbert Wieners? How many others are lost because they sit alone in a large (or small) high school, with no one to talk to because no one can speak their language? Since genius IQ may be one in a million, there aren't likely to be two around!

Four hundred outstanding men and women of the twentieth century, many of whom were geniuses, were included in Victor and Mildred Goertzel's *Cradles of Eminence*, which contained such names as Jane Addams, the Barrymores, Alexander Graham Bell, Enrico Caruso, George Washington Carver, Cézanne, Charles Chaplin, Winston Churchill, Freud, Hitler, Ibsen, Helen Keller, John D. Rockefeller, and Woodrow Wilson. Three out of five of these 400 "loathed" school (the classroom); this was an "international phenomenon," however — not just one confined to the United States.

Grieg, the composer, stood under a rainspout so his teacher would send him home; Sigrid Undset "hated school intensely"; William Saroyan said he "resented school, but never resented learning."

The enthusiasm with which gifted children and gifted parents (but not always the parents who are not gifted themselves) seize upon special programs such as independent study and individualized instruction indicates that Saroyan's attitude is that of most exceptionally intelligent students. So is the fact that these boys and girls, though bored in school, often avidly read books supposedly far too "difficult" for their age group. (I was a good little girl, ordinarily, but *I sneaked books out of the adult section of the library!*)

In addition to being bored in school—and often *because* they were—many of the outstanding 400 were also considered stupid. Thomas Edison said he was always at the foot of his class! And Albert Einstein was considered dull by both his teachers and his parents. Rachmaninoff changed poor grades (1s) on his report card to good ones (4s) at a conservatory of music. Pablo Picasso refused to do anything at school but paint, so it is less surprising that he did not do well; what surprised everyone was that he had no trouble in passing difficult entrance examinations for higher education. This was true of a number of other geniuses who did poorly in school.

Besides reading on their own, many of these children were taught by their parents. There was no parent-tutored boy or girl among the four hundred who was not grateful for the experience, the authors said.

When our youngest son became ill, at eleven, we taught him at home. I was supposed to be teaching him "the seventh grade," and his principal gave me all the standard textbooks. But the doctors had told us that Johnny had an incurable disease, so we wanted him to learn everything he could learn in the "fifteen months" they said he might have.

That is why I did not bother much about the textbooks. He took one look at the seventh grade math problems and said disappointedly, "There's nothing new."

Johnny had had an outstanding young teacher in the sixth grade who gave him some advanced math that I did not understand. I wasn't much help in that realm, but we let him do algebra.

"The high schools don't like us to start algebra in junior high," the principal told us, "because it's supposed to be taught in high school."

But Johnny was doing all the seventh grade review problems with no errors, so the principal gave us the eighth grade book; this one had a few new odds and ends but still no algebra. I sometimes wonder, when it comes to bright children, if we really need a junior high school at all. Perhaps the answer is to use it as a catching-up place for children who have not yet learned to read well and who need the review in arithmetic, with some time for "fun subjects." Those who didn't need the review could then go from elementary school to four-year high school. I can just hear the Education Establishment exploding at such an idea; never mind, it's just one of those creative brainstorms. It is true, however, that no one can ever quite decide what to do with junior high. Boys and girls in the same city may go from eighth grade to freshman year in high school or from ninth grade to the sophomore year. The new idea of middle schools has run into even more confusion—shall the middle school cover fifth grade? Ninth grade?

At the end of Johnny's year at home, although he had worked only a few hours a day at his leisure, instead of from 8 to 3, and with a teacher who had to do little more than make suggestions, Johnny was invited to graduate with the eighth grade class. Possibly the compassionate principal just felt that he would like to graduate, although the decision was based on achievement tests with a battery median in the tenth grade (10.2), ranging from 7.6 in science (a neglected area in our family background) to 12.3 in study skills, and eleventh-grade math.

But by this time Johnny had achieved a remission from his disease, which was to last nearly four years; it gave him the chance to join his older brother on the high school tennis team, to get three varsity letters and to win the Harvard award for most outstanding boy in his junior class. He was a senior, and had just won a state scholarship to the college of his choice on the basis of his college entrance exam scores when the medicine finally stopped working.

He had said, "I want to do every single thing that I can do." And he had. He hadn't wasted any of his precious time.

In teaching him this way, not worrying about the conventions as most parents, teachers and administrators feel they must, I came to a few conclusions about why school is "boring" for so many children.

It is not usually the teacher's fault so much as it is the system she or he is forced to conform to. Even a great teacher is handcuffed by administrative rules (if she has a "nonsupportive" principal) and by the material she has to "cover" (the textbook, no matter how colorful, with its standardized "things to learn"). (An extremely interesting book about texts is Hillel Black's *The American Schoolbook*, William Morrow Company, 1967.) Johnny dutifully did the exercises at the end of each chapter in his social studies book, but he hated it until I let him loose in the encyclopedia and any other books in the house or at the library on the same general subject as the textbook. Then he got interested, because *there was no end* to what he could find out about — China, for instance; China is a fascinating subject, but not when all you know about it is the capital, imports and exports, and a few other odds and ends.

A highly gifted eleventh grader in a recent study was asked what he enjoyed least in school. Reading textbooks was at the top of his list. "I just can't get through something that's boring, and textbooks are boring."

So we decided Johnny had done enough exercises, and could just skim through the book and pick out the things he wanted to know more about. This resulted, of course, in his knowing more geography and history than his classmates at school ever learned. And since we also dispensed with memorizing facts for tests, which he would forget as soon as the tests were taken, he could use that wasted rote-memory time to find out many more details which he did remember because they interested him.

Another stupid thing that I had been doing for years, even in teaching college Freshman Composition, was the assignment of "theme topics." Teachers and textbook writers have been figuring out lockstep composition subjects without thinking about it simply because this is the way it has always been done. The subjects seldom fit any of the students, let alone all of them. With ingenuity, a good student can twist them around to "where he's at," but most students just sigh and hammer it out. The results are nearly always wordy, say-nothing pages that bore both writer and reader. English teachers assign these papers, I suppose, in order to have something to correct the spelling and punctuation of!

I decided not to do this to Johnny, even though it was what the

English curriculum prescribed. Perhaps it takes a very special reason to give you the courage to break the rules, but all teachers should start realizing that *every child who is bored in school* is a visible reminder to do something about it. Teachers like Jonathan Kozol (*Death at an Early Age*) in the Boston schools and James Herndon (*The Way It Spozed to Be*) in San Francisco had the courage, and succeeded in teaching children who never had learned before. But these gifted educators were fired for not conforming to the pattern that has been boring most of us since we were in the first grade.

"Write anything you want to," I told Johnny, "but write one page in your composition book every day."

"What'll I write about?" he asked, as any class would if a teacher suddenly took away her support.

"Look out the window and write what you see. Write what you're thinking . . ."

"Like, 'This is a stupid assignment,'" he said, grinning.

"Absolutely," I told him. "Be honest. That's the only way you'll write anything original. Otherwise you just copy down what you're supposed to think: somebody else's ideas."

I'm not sure these were my exact words—this was years ago—but I am sure of what Johnny wrote, because I still have his fifteen-cent composition book.

He wrote narratives about a camping trip and a train trip, several descriptions of landscapes ("out the window"), some criticisms of TV shows and books he read, some suggestions for educational innovations, a couple of poems, considerable sports-reporting on World Series and football games, some letters to his brother-in-law in the Air Force (when I said that would count), and then about half-way through the notebook he started writing *stories* and stopped confining himself to a page a day. He let loose with his imagination and the first ones were pretty wild, but they got better and better.

The last one was a satire on Westerns, "Show-Down at Gallows City," and it begins, "The saloon door opened, and in came Saloon man Sam. Counting his 2 pint hat, he was 5'6" and didn't look any too kind. Sam was a stranger in town, Gallows City that is. I want a milk! said Sam, coming to the counter. Everybody in the saloon started laughing. One man said, give the baby his milk. Sam was good-natured enough to let him off with a black eye."

I didn't "correct" his notebook, I just enjoyed it with him, but sometimes I would tell him something like, in this case, how to punctuate dialog. It's better to point out one thing at a time, rather than a hodge-podge of different errors on every piece of writing. It's more memorable — and less stuffy.

The surprising thing is, when one looks it over, one sees that Johnny actually did write the very things a teacher usually suggests: narrative, description, autobiography, letters, literary criticism, even book reports, sportswriting, poetry, and short stories. But he did each one *when it was on his mind*, not when he had no ideas on that subject that day.

Our spelling method, which resulted in Johnny scoring an 11.9 on the achievement tests, was very simple. I gave him orally a 500-word list from a college handbook, and checked the ones he got wrong. The next day we went over the checked words and narrowed it down some more. We were through with spelling by the end of the first month. I understand the current method of teaching spelling is based on rules, not lists, but I wonder if that doesn't waste some time? Of course, spelling comes easily to some people and doesn't come at all to others just as bright. And somebody can always correct your spelling, so it really isn't as important as what you have to say.

Reading and writing should be fun, and we teachers, of all people, have been taking the joy out of both. We shouldn't assign "book reports" on a limited choice of "classics," either ancient or modern, or the kids will hate books. Indeed, book reports should take on the excitement of discovery — what phrases did the author use to describe the main character(s); what events built the personality of the protagonist; rewrite the climax of the story so that the ending differs; who-what in the story do you admire? Try these questions with *Charlotte's Web* or *The Hobbit* and see if the resulting book report is not a clear indication of what a student has learned.

The Reading is FUN-da-mental program (RIF) founded by Mrs. Margaret McNamara of Washington, D.C., has as its major purpose developing motivation to read. The program operates in disadvantaged areas on the theory that a child should have the fun of picking out "a book of his own." The book that the child selects does indeed become his own to read and keep. The idea works. RIF provides matching funds for public and non-profit agencies to make multiple reading materials available to children. For information write: RIF, Smithsonian Institute, Washington, D.C. 20560.

"Forming a child's taste" by force-feeding *our* choices (or even the same "famous" books that bored us when we were in school) is more likely to make the child dislike good books than like them.

Johnny didn't like to read (this has made the book I wrote about him popular with children who don't like to read), but when I let him read anything he wanted he found *some* books he liked: Tolkien's books, Schulz's *Peanuts* — he had a collection of them, and made up a hilarious Peanuts Dictionary — Sinclair Lewis's *Arrowsmith*, books by tennis players, and books on chess. Books can both form and reflect a child's interests.

There are so many fascinating things to learn that there is no excuse for boring children. In fact, it sometimes seems as if schools go out of their way to do just that. Boredom is at the root of the dropout problem in high schools, and it isn't confined to students with low academic potential; it has been estimated that as many as half of the gifted drop out of high school and college. This doesn't mean that some of these dropouts don't achieve success, or even eminence, in later life, as Dr. and Mrs. Goertzel's work shows.

But if our system of compulsory schooling is not *helping* people to achieve this success, but actually holding them back from their later contributions to society, then what is our excuse for making them waste so many years "getting educated?"

Mr. David Tyack, Professor of Education and History at Stanford University, in the winter 1977 *Carnegie Quarterly*, suggests that the historical commitment to help youngsters that is implied in compulsory schooling laws is a value worth keeping. "What we should be questioning anew," he says, "is the way we meet this obligation to the young. . . . schools should no longer insist that youngsters merely spend time in class, but should make sure that youngsters develop their potential to be effective participants in society and to share in the benefits of the good life." Meeting this goal, he says, may call for not only offering traditional classes but also for providing work and other educational experiences. (*Carnegie Quarterly*, Winter 1977, Carnegie Corporation of New York, 437 Madison Avenue, New York, New York 10022.)

If the boys and girls who teach themselves, are tutored, or participate in innovative programs are enjoying learning, while the majority of U.S. schoolchildren are bored, what should we do about it?

It is time to make school an alive, vital place where the excitement and joy of learning abound. Some learning is tedious and not much fun. A child's tolerance of the less interesting tasks, however, is increased when he knows that the necessary disciplines of a new language or science or math course will open up vistas of knowledge he will never tire of exploring.

SPECIAL INTEREST REFERENCE:

Holt, John. *What Do I Do Monday.* New York: E. P. Dutton, 1970. In this and his other books, Mr. Holt draws the curtain of conventional teaching and shows how much children can enjoy being on the stage of learning. He doesn't address himself to special education for the gifted, but his ideas are valuable for all children — and teachers.

San Diego schools are supporting voluntary busing to cluster schools
as an alternative to compulsory busing. Marilyn De La Torre teaches
piano in one of these schools. (Photo courtesy of San Diego Schools)

Photography is an intriguing activity for bright students. (Photo
courtesy of San Diego Schools)

A well-stocked resource center is an essential part of any program for the gifted. (Photo courtesy of San Diego Schools)

Owenita Sanderlin, author, talks to children about writing books. (Photo courtesy of San Diego Schools)

7
Should Students Be Grouped by Ability?
Are You a Robin or a Bluebird?

Issues:

Does ability grouping result in an intellectual elite?
What effect does ability grouping have on the non-gifted?
Is there such a thing as a homogeneous group?
How well can teachers handle groups of varying abilities?
How should decisions be made to group by ability or not?
Does ability grouping result in greater achievement?
What is the effect of ability grouping on students, parents, teachers?

MONTAIGNE (16th century): *Such as according to our common way of thinking undertake, with one and the same lesson, and the same measure of direction, to instruct several boys of differing and unique capacities, are infinitely mistaken; and 'tis no wonder, if in a whole multitude of scholars, there are not found above two or three who bring away any good account of their time and discipline.*

JAMES BRYANT CONANT (scientist, educator, former Harvard President, 1959): *Students should be grouped by ability, subject by subject.*

(In 1967 follow-up study): *At the time my first study was made . . . "ability grouping" was a highly controversial subject. As I then recorded, I have met competent teachers who argued vigorously for the heterogeneous grouping in all classes. . . . Other teachers were equally certain that justice cannot be done to either the bright student or the slow reader if both receive instruction in the same class. The controversy seems to have subsided . . . for 96.5 percent of the principals [in 2000 high schools] responded affirmatively to the following question: Do you group students by ability in one or more academic subjects?*

LOUISE BATES AMES (1967): *Children of superior endowment should certainly be grouped with others of similar endowment in a top group.*

JOHN HOLT (1969): *I am altogether opposed to any kind of ability grouping in school.*

WILLIAM GLASSER (educator, writer, M.D., 1969): *Tracking, or homogeneous grouping by ability is bad not only because of its effect on the students; it also has an insidious and destructive effect upon teachers.*

NEIL POSTMAN AND CHARLES WEINGARTNER (teachers and writers, 1969): . . . *there is hardly a school in the country that has not organized children into groups labeled "dumb" so that both their teachers and they can know exactly what they "are."*

MARK R. LOHMAN (a UC-Riverside professor testifying before a Senate Committee on Equal Educational Opportunity, as reported in *Los Angeles Times*, November 14, 1971): *Schools grouping pupils by ability tests are signalling to the lower level students a clear, devastating social message which will change his life. "Those guys are better than I am. I'm not going anywhere," a student will think, then give up and accept his fate.*

SIDNEY P. MARLAND, JR. (U.S. Commissioner of Education, in a report to Congress, 1971): *Clear support for special groupings was found in New York, in the Major Work Classes in Cleveland, in Los Angeles, and in numerous other locales. Participants showed improvement not only in academic areas but also in personal and social areas.*

JOHN I. GOODLAD (noted for his work on nongraded schools, 1965): *Fifth graders commonly read . . . at levels ranging all the way from*

*the second or third grade to the ninth or tenth. . . . [The child] can
be in the fifth grade for arithmetic computation, the . . . seventh for
spelling . . . the eighth for word meaning . . . and the tenth for
language and yet be officially registered in the sixth grade. . . .
However uneven his attainments, there is a group within the open
room working on his level in each subject, and a teacher to go with it.
If he learns rapidly, he can move from week to week to a group at a
more advanced level of achievement.*

HIGHLY GIFTED 11th GRADER (1978): *The smart kids should be
grouped together.*

HIGHLY GIFTED 3rd GRADER (1978): *There should be different
groups for different kids at different speeds.*

GEORGE I. THOMAS and JOSEPH CRESCIMBENI (1966): *Every pupil in
the heterogeneous class can benefit from the stimulation applied by a
few extremely bright pupils. Much has been said about the waste of
intellect when gifted students are left in heterogeneous classrooms.
But . . . these pupils have a great deal to gain from working in an atmosphere where they can excel and be acknowledged as leaders.*

JOHN CURTIS GOWAN and E. PAUL TORRANCE (1971): *. . . it is what
happens in class, and not how it is grouped, that counts.*

The controversy has been constant, is, and will continue to rage as
long as one believes in the validity of generalizations.

It is interesting to note that while conservative opinion has turned
more and more toward ability grouping, an arrangement it formerly
opposed, many radical or innovative thinkers are now turning away
from it.

Jean Piaget, the Swiss psychologist who carries weight with education people in both the old camp and the new, says that *everyone has
constantly urged that schooling should be adapted to the child.*

It should be hard to find anyone who would not agree with this
statement in theory; yet in practice the majority of schools are still
working against it. We still support education *en masse:* we teach
children of the same age the same things in the same room even if we
have to organize the kids into "ability groups" to accomplish this purpose—only we never do accomplish it.

Reading is the best example of the failure of this time-honored system of grouping: it goes way back to the robins, the blue jays, and the orioles. But many gifted children learn to read before they get to school, some as early as two years old, and this formerly frowned-upon practice is now being encouraged by some authorities. I hope the new young first-grade teachers are happier about it than they used to be!

Other bright children do *not* learn to read even when they get to school because they are bored by the content of their books or the structured methods of teaching reading—at the rate of about one sentence per child per day, in "recitation." Gifted teachers have always managed to get around this regimentation by creative methods, but with large classes and no teachers' aides they find it hard to find time enough to tutor the children who most need help in learning how to read, and at the same time, to keep the fast learners interested.

A ray of hope for this malady is the Early Childhood Education movement of the last several years, which requires a larger ratio of adults to children—one adult to each ten children in California. This additional help should pay learning dividends for both the slower moving child and the child who mainly needs encouragement and opportunity to move ahead on his own.

It has been said that as many as fifty percent of all children get to high school without the reading skills needed to tackle their high school subjects. This should be all the indication we need that the traditional reading methods do not work. When teachers (in the old-fashioned-type schools that still predominate) divide their classes into birds, flowers, A and B groups, or whatever "secret" code they use, not a kid in the room is so "dumb" that he doesn't know he is in the slow, bottom, or inferior group, and that the other kids are better readers than he is.

This is why I could never see why parents and teachers continue to insist that it's more "democratic" (or kinder) to keep "A" kids in classes with "F" kids *of the same age*. It seems to me that it is undemocratic, and bad for the slower learner's self-confidence. Robert Rosenthal and Lenore Jacobson conducted an experiment with a different type of grouping, reporting on it in *Pygmalion in the Classroom*. They told teachers that some of their children had the potential to develop more rapidly than others, even though this was not a fact. The children were not told, just the teachers, but what happened was that the pupils with "potential" did in fact develop faster than the others simply because the teachers expected them to, and treated them as if they could. They gained an average of 24.4 IQ points in one year while the control group gained only 12.

There are various studies done over the years that support the evidence cited above. It is axiomatic that if we expect our children to be "good," to be responsible, they are likely to meet that expectation, at least to the degree that they are developmentally and intellectually able. A classic story that has traveled among teaching professionals concerns the principal who gave a teacher her class list with numbers following each name. The teacher assumed that the numbers were the IQ scores of the children. Since they were all in the high 120's and 130's she taught them as though they were very able, indeed gifted, students. They performed well under this style of tutelage and achieved high scores in the semester tests. Had the teacher known that the numbers were in truth the students' locker numbers she might not have used the same approach in teaching them.

Ability grouping in age-grouped classrooms also wastes a great deal of time in duplicated effort; a second-grade fast group, for instance, may be reading at the same level as a fourth-grade middle group. And pupils who don't know how to read at all are commonly given the same amount of time as children who could go off in a corner and read all by themselves if only they didn't have to sit in a circle and, in the name of egalitarianism, "recite" at a snail's pace.

The notion that there is any such thing as a homogeneous group is probably fallacious. I believe it was John Goodlad who said that there is no such thing as a homogeneous group; even a group of one is not a homogeneous group. A child may have a full-scale score on a Wechsler of 140, but there is nothing homogeneous about his ability. He might be, for example, a good reader but a poor mathematician or the converse, or his verbal skills might be unusually good, but he lacks problem-solving skills. None of us are equally adept or inept at all things.

So, the concept of homogeneity may be in question unless we're speaking about milk or salad oil.

I have never forgotten my first-grade teacher, nor even her name.

Miss Applewhite made first grade a joy. I suppose she initially taught us all together—I don't remember when I learned how to read—but the minute we knew how (and it is a skill that "happens" to you suddenly, sometimes), we were allowed to go off and "just read" one book after another, putting a bookmark in the page where we left off each day. I remember the first story I ever read was "The Little Red Hen," and that I read twenty-six books in first grade. It doesn't seem possible we could have regressed in an area of education as important as reading, does it? And yet—fifty percent of all children get to high school with insufficient reading skills. How many of our dropouts are frustrated nonreaders?

Ability grouping as a phrase seems to be used to mean different things, which may be one reason different educators and community members do not agree as to whether it's a good thing or not. Another word sometimes used as a synonym is *tracking* or *laning*. According to the principal of a junior high school I visited, he could do nothing for the gifted in his school because the community was against any form of tracking or ability grouping; he simply could not set up any special classes. A group of new seventh-graders who had been identified as gifted and belonged to a "cluster" in elementary school were disappointed that there was nothing like this in junior high; it had been a successful experience, filling them with enthusiasm for learning—freely, and at their own speed.

A common problem with gifted programs is that as children move from school to school, whether from elementary to junior high or to another part of the country, they may lose benefits they have come to enjoy. This is why we must fight for the cause of these special children who will be so valuable (or dangerous!) to our society in the future, and we must do this in every state of the Union.

Conservative community members who believe in states' rights and local control of education should scrutinize their own interests more closely, and ask themselves, "Do we want the gifted children in our community to be able to compete with the gifted in other states?"

There is an undeniable necessity for outstanding adults, isn't there? Then why must we try so hard to hide, even to destroy, those same gifts in our children?

Opponents of homogeneous classes do have some good arguments. That slower learners need the enthusiasm of good students in their classes is one of the best objections to ability grouping; another is that bright children may suffer if they are put into a homogeneous group where there are "all chiefs and no Indians," where the less aggressive may become followers rather than the leaders they would have been in a regular class.

When Johnny was in the fifth grade we lived in a suburban district where there happened to be many bright children, and as a "capable but shy" student (an earlier teacher comment) he was a follower: he contributed to, but did not edit, the school paper, and played left field on the baseball team. The next year when we moved to a rural area he was editor of the paper and captain of the baseball team. We felt both experiences were good ones; perhaps he would not have done so well at school two if he had not been associated with the enthusiastic children in school one. And he was happy in both schools.

Another difficulty for students in accelerated or honors classes is that it is harder to make top grades, which in high school are essential for getting into college, and winning scholarships. It might be helpful if we could abolish grades, especially in gifted classes, but as long as the major universities and colleges in the country use grades as the major criterion for admission, there is not much hope for change here. A survey of high school students in a California school who had taken honors or accelerated classes at some time and elected to "drop out" showed that 80% of the dropouts cited concern over getting high grades and "working too hard" as their reasons. A good teacher friend — one of those rare creative, unthreatened teachers, had a unique approach to assigning grades in his Advanced Placement English classes. He informed students on the first day of class that they all had A's for the semester. He hastened to inform them that they could lose their A's if they didn't maintain the standards of which he and their counselors knew they were capable. Hard work and effort were important elements in the class, but the students knew where they stood.

The controversy over ability grouping remains unsettled. As a debate coach in competitive tournaments I learned that given a good question, either the affirmative or the negative can *win*. I also learned that of five highly competent judges in a debate final, three can decide for one team and two for the other. Finally, I learned that judges are sometimes prejudiced, and that one prejudiced judge could therefore decide who wins!

From that perspective let us admit that there are good arguments both for and against ability grouping. Both systems of grouping for instruction can be useful and appropriate, depending on the conditions and circumstances. In an Advanced Placement Calculus class, for example, the students need to share some common talent in mathematics. Even when they share this talent, however, the teacher must spend more time with some while others move ahead at a more rapid rate. Additionally, the able math students enjoy the challenge that other students of comparable ability provide. If one wants to become a better tennis player, playing people who are less skilled does not help much. It is better to seek out those who will challenge and extend one's skill. We must not overlook, however, the pleasure and satisfaction that comes from "social" tennis. When we group ourselves for the purpose of enjoying a personal interaction with others, we do not expect to become better tennis players, but rather to become richer persons from this human interaction.

In February 1972, at a conference attended by leaders in gifted education from all over the country, William Vassar of Connecticut said sensibly, "Ability grouping is neither good nor bad; it depends on the program." He feels that a policy of semi-separation is good, with the gifted spending some time in general classes and some in special classes.

In our elementary schools, where our expectations are both in learning the basic skills and in learning to relate, enjoy, and respect others, we can meet most effectively these expectations by grouping various ability levels together. At the high school level, teaching the content of the various subject areas — achieving some degree of specialization — tends to be our expectation. Grouping by ability, at least in some areas, may be the best way of meeting this expectation. In the absence of really homogeneous grouping and given the exceedingly difficult task of teaching chidren whose talents, interests, and motivation are all over the map, we must reform our elementary and secondary schools into places where every child can learn at his own speed. We need to find or retrain enough teachers who can teach in new and better ways, many of which have already been devised. Finally, if we can give such teachers the help they need from assistants and teachers' aides, and principals and superintendents who will support their ideas, even give them more ideas, then special groups or classes or schools for the gifted may not be needed.

Let's talk about some of the good new ideas that may render "ability grouping," with its faults as well as its virtues, unnecessary.

Above all, there is individualization of instruction. In *Creative Teaching*, I wrote a case study of an elementary school, Silver Gate in San Diego, which was running a successful pilot project funded by the school district. The principle behind this technique, which is becoming more and more widely used throughout the country, is the same as that of the old-fashioned one-room "little red schoolhouse" (and a few exist today), where the pupils ranged in both age and ability from primary to college prep, and one teacher had to teach them all. Obviously, she had to give each child whatever he needed, whether it was how to read, or how to do algebra or Latin or get into college. She took them from "where they were at" to where they wanted to go.

Individualized instruction has been poorly defined and, consequently, poorly understood as it has grown in popular acclaim over the past few years. (It is probably more correctly defined as personalized instruction.) Individualized instruction is not one "teacher" for each child. It is not twenty-five children at twenty-five different places in a math book. But rather it is an individual assessment of each child—his achievement in each of the subject areas, what motivates him (makes him care about learning), his work style, and the manner in which he works and plays with others. Knowing these things about each child, the teacher sets about structuring the learning experiences. (Yes, informal instruction requires very careful structuring!) There may indeed be some "one-on-one" instruction, there may also be small group instruction, the members of which change with the concepts being learned. It should be noted that even in the most pure of informal learning classrooms there are times when the entire group learns together. Under circumstances such as these the joys of learning become a reality for all children and a rich reward for the hard-working teacher.

Many new mechanical aids for individualized instruction have been and are being devised, such as teaching machines, computer consoles, programmed textbooks, tapes, earphones and other audio-visual aids, language labs, and educational television. But even more important are the new teaching techniques: the use of teachers' aides, team teaching, independent study (including contract learning or individually prescribed instruction), pupil-tutors, and various combinations of these.

Almost indispensable to individualization of instruction are teachers' aides and assistants, including part-time parents, college students and community volunteers, especially those who have special skills to offer, such as one who can teach fourth-year math where there is no full-time teacher available. Such special teachers (who may or may not be paid) are called paraprofessionals, and they act as librarians, tutor small groups, and so on. Parent assistants are also employed to do clerical work.

Students tell us of the delight they experience in being tutors for other students. In the Palo Alto survey of highly gifted students, they often make reference to the thrill of teaching someone else and how much better the tutor understands a complicated idea when he explains it to another. A highly gifted fifth-grader responded to the question, "What is the most important thing that happened in school today?" by saying, "Helping a second grader learn to read and do math better." In schools where peer or cross-age tutoring are a regular part of the school operation, the feelings of children for each other are warm, respectful, and familial.

For detailed information on how to use aides, see Betty Atwell Wright's *Teacher Aides to the Rescue*, New York: John Day, 1969; Frank Riessman's *Up From Poverty*, New York: Harper & Row, 1968; or *Teacher Assistants*, by Mel H. Robb, Columbus, Ohio: Charles E. Merrill Pub. Co., 1969.

"Team teaching" is a phrase coined in 1957 when this innovation, now widely accepted, was initiated in a Lexington, Masschusetts high school. Simply, it is the use of a master teacher or two, with one or more assistants, to share a class or classes. The concept lends itself to many variations, such as the more complex "pontoon" system, or the Independent Studies "school within a school" with two teachers, one a math and science teacher and the other specializing in the humanities, sharing a group of gifted students for a large part of the school day.

Computer-assisted instruction is another way of individualizing the basic work to fit each pupil; so far it's limited in use for financial and organizational reasons, and because while there are computers that can "teach" (the hardware), we don't yet have enough good teaching materials (the software) to stock the computers.

However, given a computer terminal connecting a distant elementary school to a central computer, we *can* teach a child the basics of a subject like arithmetic or a language, individually, and, as nearly as the teacher can determine from his performance, on the machine, at his own pace. The work of Patrick Suppes has been outstanding in this field, and it seems likely that further progress will be made. We can hope that computers will give teachers more time to do the things for kids that machines can't do.

Ideally, with computers or similar "programmed learning" in books, gifted children could gobble up the basics in any subject and forge ahead as far as their minds could take them; it could save them much valuable time. For slow learners, the main value is that they can take as long as they need to learn thoroughly, to understand before they go on. It also means there would be no need for comparative grades on "report cards." Both gifted and average or retarded learners could get "all A's" up to the limit of their capacity to learn in each subject; the only difference would be in the time it takes.

In any kind of individualized or individually prescribed instruction or contract learning, there are no "ability groups." It's every child for himself. It is generally conceded that anyone can learn more if he has a tutor; individualized teaching in heterogeneous, *nongraded* schools would be the nearest we could come to a tutorial system, and still maintain the added advantage of the beneficial social experiences our public schools have unquestionably provided for our children.

So it isn't a question of whether ability grouping is good or bad. The way most schools are still set up, it's probably a necessary evil, but we don't have to settle for any kind of evil. There are too many sensible solutions to the problem of how, in a school system that serves all our children, we can best serve each one of them.

There is no excuse for not making use of these new and widely tested ideas except for apathy and inertia, or unthinking emotionalism — in a word, prejudice. But perhaps it is the "early days" yet; perhaps we should continue to try out these techniques with the children who are most likely to benefit from them, and to show how they can work for others: our gifted "pioneers."

One of the bonuses inherent in an evaluation of the outstanding gifted programs the state of Illinois is working on is precisely this "spillover" effect. "Many of the materials and techniques introduced in gifted programs," they note, "have been utilized in other classes as well."

Dr. Paul Plowman, Project Director of the Gifted and Talented Management Team for the state of California, includes in his evaluation of their 1976-1977 Federal Project, "Development of Teaching Competencies—Gifted and Talented" the comment, "Thus, in addition to facilitating skills necessary for differentiating instruction for the gifted, the project had a desirable 'spreading effect' of value to the regular child and to the personal lives of participants." This is one of the real satisfactions which comes from working in the area of the gifted.

Ability grouping may be one of the most serious disadvantages of gifted programs in that it may lead to elitism. Yet students, parents and teachers agree that grouping ability provides a unique opportunity for an intellectually stimulating class.

We must conclude that no grouping procedure is ideal. We cannot look solely to a sorting system to resolve the issues of how best to teach gifted kids. We must examine the expectations we have for a class, or experience, and then design the instruction so that we realize that expectation. And, of course, the key factor in the whole controversy is the teacher. The skilled, gifted teacher is one who is able to deal with various kinds of groupings. When a teacher knows and cares about students and knows and cares about the tasks to be learned, then he can pace himself and the learning options so as to accommodate the differing abilities of the students. A gifted high school student, when asked how he would organize school so he could learn best said, "It doesn't matter how students are grouped or whether the classroom is arranged in rows or in a circle, it's the teacher who creates the setting."

Individualized instruction must be our ultimate goal, however we achieve it.

SPECIAL INTEREST REFERENCES:

"What About Elitist High Schools?", William Raspberry. One of seven articles that are special features on the gifted and talented in the Jan./Feb., 1976 *Today's Education*. Mr. Raspberry, columnist for the *Washington Post*, discusses from student and teacher comments the dilemma in which gifted students find themselves in the anti-intellectual atmosphere of big city high schools.

"My Son the Linguist and Reader," by Sam Sebesta. *English Teacher Journal*, February, 1968. This is a delightful article which carries a big punch. Mr. Sebesta feels that the beginning reading task is more than matching sets of sounds to letters; it is developing an awareness of what reading is — stories, words, sentences — and what it is for — understanding.

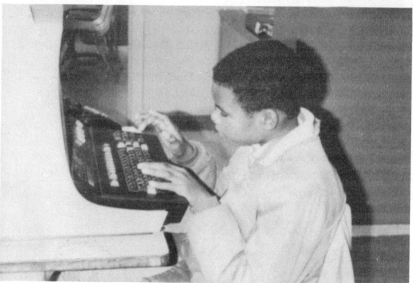

In an Independent Study Center in Palo Alto, Mrs. Joan Targ coordinates various programs for the academically talented. Among them are chess seminars and computer programming. (Photo courtesy of Joan Targ)

8
Acceleration - Or Enrichment?
Is Faster Better or Is More Better?

Issues:

Is acceleration harmful to the child?
What are alternatives to acceleration?
What is enrichment?
Can a teacher provide enough enrichment for a really bright child?
Is it possible to accelerate a child in some areas but not in others?

MRS. NORMAL: *"Your child was pushed ahead!''*

MRS. BRIGHT: *"It seems to me the child who gets promoted when he hasn't learned to read yet is the one who is pushed ahead."*

SIDNEY P. MARLAND, JR. (1971): *Fifty percent of public school educators opposed acceleration, despite research evidence that acceleration is beneficial at every level from kindergarten to college.*

JEROME BRUNER (1960): *Ideally, schools should allow students to go ahead in different subjects as rapidly as they can. But the administrative problems that are raised when one makes such an arrangement possible are almost inevitably beyond the resources that schools have available for dealing with them. The answer will probably lie in some modification or abolition of the system of grade levels in some subjects, notably mathematics, along with a program of course enrichment in other subjects.*

LEWIS TERMAN AND MELITA ODEN (1947): *It is our opinion that children of 135 IQ or higher should be promoted sufficiently to permit college entrance by the age of seventeen at the latest, and . . . a majority . . . at sixteen. Acceleration to this extent is especially desirable for those who plan to complete two or more years of graduate study in preparation for a professional career.*

LOUISE BATES AMES (1967): *Enrichment rather than pushing ahead is our recommendation for most highly superior children.*

LEWIS TERMAN AND MELITA ODEN (1966): *Unfortunately, the so-called enrichment often amounts to little more than a quantitative increase of work on the usual level.*

WILLIAM VASSAR (in a speech in San Diego, 1972): *Too many kids are getting nothing more than more of the same.*

GEORGE I. THOMAS AND JOSEPH CRESCIMBENI (1966) *If the objective is to get these pupils into college at sixteen or seventeen, the same results can be achieved by accelerating the curriculum rather than the pupil.*

JOHN I. GOODLAD (in "The Schools vs. Education," *Saturday Review*, April 19, 1969): *No need . . . to confine teaching to the hours between 9 in the morning and 3 in the afternoon, nor to delay certain subjects until high school or college.*

RUTH STRANG (1960): *A good plan seems to be to complete the first three grades in two years and the three junior high grades in two years. Some children who develop rapidly in high school may profit by advanced placement programs which enable them to save one year of college.*

ALVIN C. EURICH (1969): *. . . early admission to college . . . began in 1951 in twelve colleges and has now been extended to many more on the basis of satisfactory results. . . . admission with advanced standing [having taken some college courses while in high school] . . . too, has proved effective. . . . Both of these methods tend to reduce boredom and wasteful human activity.*

CHARLES SILBERMAN (1970): . . . in the elementary grades, an able student can be absent from school for an entire week and, quite literally, catch up with all he missed in a single morning.

GEORGE I. THOMAS AND JOSEPH CRESCIMBENI (1966): . . . *many teachers and . . . administrators are opposed to acceleration programs as a matter of principle. They will argue that the accelerated students will not be mature enough, but beyond this generalization they tend to get lost in vague generalities that have been refuted time and time again.*

JOHN CURTIS GOWAN AND GEORGE DEMOS (1964): *Somewhere between 1930 and 1933, coincident with the depression and extending on until the end of World War II, there . . . was a de-emphasis on matters . . . related to gifted children. Acceleration was damned and grouping ostracized. . . . [many] of our present educators, who were in training at the time, received their indoctrination against special education for the able.*

ROBERT F. DEHAAN (psychology professor and specialist in the study of acceleration, 1963): *When students become excited about education (as they usually do in accelerated learning programs), when they begin to see the importance of learning, when a school emphasizes achievement and develops a tradition of excellence, a new dimension is added to school life . . . respect for the realm of the intellect.*

GIFTED 12TH GRADER (1977): *AP classes* [Advanced Placement] *make good fresh hamburger out of sacred cows.*

HIGH SCHOOL SOPHOMORE IN A GIFTED PROGRAM (overheard, 1972): *My educational objectives? I want to learn everything about everything!*

JEAN PIAGET (1969): *Those individuals who are most gifted, and of most possible use to society may waste months or years of their life at precisely that age when the new ideas that will shape their future careers are taking place within them.*

Perhaps acceleration is the wrong word.

For too long we have been *decelerating* millions of children who could have learned much more than they did learn, and in a much shorter time. We have spent billions of property-tax dollars to keep elementary and secondary boys and girls who were ready to go on to college in our schools for from one to three years longer than they needed to be there. This experience either bored them or conventionalized their creative minds so that when they got to college their original endowment of intellectual curiosity was "turned off," perhaps for good.

We have ignored the fact that a great many children have, in fact, gone through our schools in less than thirteen years, and become successful and well-adjusted adults; we were too busy publicizing the convenient myths about immaturity, maladjustment, and emotional instability.

Certainly, there are cases of men and women who skipped grades in childhood (the only form of acceleration there was then) who blame their psychological troubles or difficulties in school on the skipped grade. Louise Bates Ames, in *Is Your Child in the Wrong Grade?* cites some of them, but she doesn't print any letters from people like my husband or myself, or some of our best friends and relatives for whom skipping a grade or two has turned out to be of benefit. That would not have supported her thesis, which is that children are sometimes not ready to do first grade work at age six, but that even the brightest six-year-olds will find plenty to challenge them in grade one and in the ensuing grades. This opinion is shared by the majority of the American public, and Mrs. Ames and the Gesell Institute of Child Development are outstanding authorities who have done much for parents and children; I venture to disagree, as do many other authorities, only in this area.

"Yes, your child is *capable* of doing the work of a higher grade," a principal of the traditional school will admit, "but in our experience, children who skip grades are bound to have emotional problems later on."

True. Don't we all?

Stories are rarely publicized of gifted children who did not skip grades; nor do we mention children of average ability who did not skip grades, yet had emotional problems in later life.

As long as objections to acceleration are based on emotional prejudices such as fear, jealousy, or anti-intellectualism in parents, teachers, or administrators, selected cases of sixteen-year-olds who have had nervous breakdowns in college can always be found to "prove" the point. My own personal citations of selected cases to make my point are just as unscientific.

So we have to turn to the many unbiased studies that have been made in this area—and widely ignored—for at least forty years. If you want ammunition, or need to be convinced, some examples of studies that concluded that acceleration does not harm children are:

Noel Keys. "Adjustment of Under Age Students in High School," *Psychological Bulletin* 32, October, 1935.

E. E. Lamson.*A Study of Young Gifted Children in High School.* Bureau of Publications, New York: Columbia University, Teachers College, 1930.

Ruthe A. Lundy. *Follow-up Study of Double Promoted Elementary School Students.* Thesis published at California State University, Hayward, 1974.

H. J. Klausmeier. "Effects of Accelerating Bright, Older Elementary Pupils: A Follow-Up," *Journal of Educational Psychology* 54, 1963.

Thelburn L. Engle. "A Study of the Effects of School Acceleration Upon the Personality and School Adjustment of High School and University Students." *Journal of Educational Psychology* 29, October 1938.

Joseph Justman, "Personal and Social Adjustments of Intellectually Gifted Accelerants and Non-accelerants in Junior High School." *School Review* 61, November, 1953 also one on their academic achievements in the same magazine 62, March, 1954.

Norman Mirman. "Are Accelerated Students Socially Maladjusted?" *Elementary School Journal* 62, February 1962.

The pros and cons of acceleration include the following points taken from the Lundy thesis previously mentioned:

Pros

1. Since the gifted child learns more rapidly than do other students, he needs to be provided with opportunities commensurate with his ability to progress. These opportunities help to place him in the grade that corresponds to his maturity level rather than his chronological age.

2. Students should not be forced to spend traditional blocks of time simply to facilitate academic bookkeeping. They should take the least time needed for desired educational attainment. Research studies indicate that there is little correlation between achievement in a given subject and the length of time devoted to its study. A gifted student should be encouraged to master a particular area at his own rate of speed.

3. Evidence indicates that the years of maximum health, physical strength and endurance, intellectual alertness and productivity, vigorous interest and enthusiasm, all come near the beginning of adult life. Terman's studies of age and achievement suggest that man's outstanding creative accomplishments come early in life more often than late. Acceleration capitalizes on this biological peak by putting an earlier end to full-time educational preparation and enables earlier entry into productive careers.

4. Children kept in classes in which they are not challenged develop attitudes and habits that may result in emotional maladjustments. The temporary difficulties that can result from being with students older and more mature may, in the long run, be less damaging than achieving below one's potential ability. Classmates who are chronological peers may or may not be intellectual or social peers.

5. Acceleration invites not only varied educational opportunities but more of them, either in a major interest or talent area or in fields unfamiliar to the student. Thus acceleration is actually a form of enrichment.

6. The period of full-time schooling has been lengthened to the point where intellectual, social, and economic "adolescence" is prolonged unduly. A year or two saved in early schooling can mean the completion of graduate study without delaying the age for marriage and self-support.

7. Fewer school years mean lower costs and substantial savings for students, their parents, schools, and communities. Any saving of a year or more for as few as one percent of the students in elementary and secondary school would mean the equivalent of thousands of additional man-years of productivity.

Cons

1. Education does not consist of neatly compartmentalized, logically organized units of learning in preordained sequences. While some skills may be developed in sequence, rich learning experiences do not necessarily come from a fixed pattern of subject matter. While it is possible to decrease time spent on particular activities, certain learnings arise only from studies in depth and breadth.

2. The boredom that breeds on lack of challenge can be eliminated in other and better ways than reducing time spent in a class.

3. Younger students may be intellectually mature, but socially and emotionally disadvantaged among older students. Opportunities for leadership in some areas may be denied students because of physical or social immaturity with older groups.

4. Acceleration deprives gifted children of opportunities for full living and learning. Bright students cannot compensate for the learnings that come from time and opportunity to think, reflect, explore, and appreciate. Creativity may be curbed by lack of leisure and by pressures to maintain rapid progress in all areas.

5. Comparability of mental age does not necessarily mean similar intellectual functioning or maturity. A six-year-old with a mental age of nine years and the nine-year-old with a mental age of nine perform qualitatively quite differently. Acceleration into an advanced grade may provide more difficult work but, in terms of the child's total educational development, may not result in more appropriate experiences.

6. Because of different maturation rates, the child's development may be quite uneven. While he might profit from accelerated experiences in one area, he may not be ready for rapid progress in others. Pressures to achieve and maintain standards of equal attainment in all areas may affect his motivation as well as his overall educational development.

7. Acceleration tends to emphasize differences in ability and to set the gifted apart from his age peers. Undesirable social and emotional behavior patterns may result from this separation.

8. When skipping occurs, serious gaps may result in the student's learning, affecting the quality of later performance. This is especially true in skill areas where there are sequential developments.

Barbara Hauck, in *The Gifted: Case Studies*, 1972, pg. 134, suggested that too often, designers of school programs for able youngsters have looked solely to administrative arrangements as a solution to problems of educating the gifted. Such arrangements are relatively ineffective without concurrent modifications of curriculum and teaching methods. A simple geographical change from one room or one school to another does not, in itself, constitute a "program" for gifted! She proposes alternative schemes: Sometimes a double promotion will solve the problem for the time being. More often, the child will work in a single area, or several areas of the curriculum with an older grade level grouping, but will remain with his or her social and chronological age peers for the rest of his school day. Some classes are composed of a "cluster" of gifted students along with another specific ability level. The cluster of gifted work at their own pace, enjoying the challenge and stimulation of other bright companions while the teacher is serving the usual number of children in the classroom.

Ms. Hauck also observes that "Popularity for an arrangement often is in conflict with research and pedagogic experience. The data on acceleration have been remarkably and consistently optimistic, but the practice of acceleration is even less frequent than the use of special classes. It is usually confined to elementary school and early placement in college."

In the past ten years, although it sometimes doesn't seem so, we have come a long way toward a more reasonable kind of education. At least we now have some better ways of teaching children, even though these ideas have not yet been put into widespread practice. We have some new answers to the old problems, such as Professor Gowan's searching question, "How do we harmonize the opposing principles of developing each individual to his maximum and at the same time provide for the greatest general good through a common education?"—which he calls a "peculiarly American problem."

When my husband and I were children (*before* 1930) the only thing the schools could do for a child who knew the material in his grade was to skip him, and they did. I can not remember that anyone ever got uptight about it.

When I was in 2-A (we had half-grades then), Ralph Waldo Emerson School was having a crowded classroom problem, possibly because of a baby boom from World War I. One day a portly, silver-haired teacher from 2-B walked in and said, "How many of you can read?"

Quite a few of us stood up; Miss Applewhite's free-reading method had worked well.

"Come with me," said Miss Noble, and we were in 2-B.

My husband had similar experiences, which resulted in his getting his Ph.D. at the age of 23, just in time: our first baby was born nine months later, during his first year of teaching. The year before that we lived on $900.

But now, two generations later, with our children's children in school, there are alternatives to skipping grades or getting "enrichment," which in our children's schools constituted nothing but more arithmetic problems or other "busy work" at the same level of learning. Outstanding among these is John Goodlad's "non-graded" school and the open or informal classrooms springing up around the country. Unfortunately, in many school districts in the United States, these alternatives are still being ignored, and in such cases skipping is still the only thing that can be done for a gifted child. I strongly advocate it for any well-adjusted, mature, physically able child who is obviously not learning anything new in the grade he is in. This is what I recommend whether a doubtful parent is uncertain to accept the school's recommendation for acceleration or whether a determined parent has to fight for it.

How lucky you are if you live in an advanced school district that is at least trying out the new ideas, including a new meaning for the word "enrichment," as well as individualized and/or non-graded schools, or plans for independent study that "accelerate the curriculum" rather than the child.

Some of the best gifted programs in the country have for a number of years been based on genuine enrichment activities and materials that "broaden and deepen" the child's knowledge; they provide different things to learn, not just more of the same. This is what an educator means when he tells you a special program, in order to receive funding from the state or federal government, must be "not quantitatively but qualitatively different."

To be called enrichment, an activity must improve a learning situation by adding something to it. It may be a deeper exploration of a topic, a special project that may or may not be related to the typical curriculum for the grade. It may be opportunities for students to apply their knowledge to more complex problems or situations, or operate at a higher level of understanding. Spencer Brown in "How to Educate the Gifted Child," *Commentary* 21: 534-41, June 1953, compares enrichment with a dog going for a walk in the country with his master. The man walks straight along the road and arrives back home in an hour and a half. The dog covers the same road and comes home at the same time. But during that hour and a half the dog has traveled not 5 but 15 miles of countryside. He has investigated openings in drains and hollow logs, and pursued his quota of squirrels. He has sniffed at strange objects, bristled and barked at other dogs, chased two real and eleven imaginary rabbits, and run, intermittently, in every direction. As a result of these experiences, his life has been enriched. He has arrived home a wiser and a stronger dog.

All the innovations mentioned in the last chapter as improvements over ability grouping (in its old sense) are equally applicable when it comes to acceleration. For convenience I'll put them in a list, although of course some of them overlap or are used in combinations. I will also add others.

Individualization of instruction.
Team teaching.
Teaching assistants or aides as tutors, librarians, etc.
Paraprofessional teachers for special subjects.
Computer-assisted instruction, educational TV and other technological innovations.
Informal classrooms.
Nongraded or ungraded schools, or combinations of grades.
Enrichment through field trips and other community resources, travelling libraries, access to laboratories and many other *genuinely* enriching activities.
Flexible scheduling.
Planned acceleration in special programs for the gifted.
Independent study (various plans).
Early admission to college.
Advanced placement, or admission to college with advanced standing, having taken college courses while in high school or by tests.
Summer school, not just for extras, but to meet requirements: result, early graduation.
Year-round school plans, with enrichment in time-off periods.
Multi-class or cross-grade groupings.
Honors and advanced classes and seminars.
Contract learning or individually prescribed instruction (IPI).
The Unit approach (building the individual curriculum around a report or study in a major-interest area).

Released-time programs (student may leave school for other cultural, educational or career-job opportunities for part of the day).

Community or other educational programs after school or on Saturdays.

Work programs (the student spends half the day or other periods of time in a career-oriented job or apprenticeship).

Self-teaching courses, including correspondence courses sometimes paid for by the school.

Programmed learning (a business school cut an accounting course from 19 to about 2 hours by programmed instruction).

Qualifying examinations for course credit; "challenge" tests.

Early entrance to school for children who can read.

Special schools for gifted or talented children.

California Project Talent (see *Final Report,* California State Department of Education, 1969) describes a successful acceleration demonstration in elementary school, based on similar programs previously tried elsewhere in the country and considered "efficient and effective." Instead of skipping a grade, with the concomitant "missed" areas of learning, second graders went to a special summer session to learn the material of the third grade, and in the fall entered fourth grade. Only 9 of the 522 accelerated children had any serious trouble in the advanced grade, and in all 9 cases their inclusion had been considered doubtful to begin with.

Interestingly, the chief "unsolved difficult problem" the study came up with was "unfavorable attitudes toward acceleration" from teachers and parents who went to school in the 1920-1940 period, and administrators who were not willing to tolerate their "incessant criticism."

In 1977 a study by Ruthe Lundy showed that children who "skipped" kindergarten (they attended the 30 days required by law) were performing academically and socially as well as or better than the nonaccelerated children.

Today more and more educators who have studied the problem are recommending one or two years of acceleration for gifted students which, as mentioned before, would save taxpayers a great deal of money!

A child's comment about his move from third to fourth grade: "Being in fourth grade is better than finding a pond full of frogs. Frogs will die, but you get to stay in fourth grade."

The list of possible ways to accelerate studies increases every year since one new concept opens up others. For example, the now widely-accepted team teaching plan, which broke into the sacred one-teacher-dominated "egg-crate" classroom in 1957, has branched out into a variety of plans. The most exciting one I've visited is the one mentioned before, the "school within a school" for a group of gifted students who spend part or all of the high school day in independent study under the leadership of two teachers, specialists in their fields of math-science and the humanities.

This idea in itself is likely to work out in various ways with different student-needs and teacher-qualifications or personalities or "teaching styles." It may take place during or after class hours. The Enfield, Connecticut, student-run social studies laboratory started in 1967 is an example. A $1000 state grant equipped the lab, and students use it enthusiastically in study periods and after school.

In San Diego and elsewhere in the country some of the junior high schools, under the enthusiastic leadership of special counselors for the gifted, have started "I. S." programs too.

The nucleus for these independent study programs may be a special room that "belongs" to the group, like the one at Morse High School, described in Chapter 5. Parents sometimes provide carpeting or the kids may piece it together with squares of different-colored rug samples. They have "water-rings" to sit in, or sometimes perch on file cabinets to have class discussions; some even use chairs! There are bookshelves, with books and magazines contributed by their dedicated teachers or the community; District Resource Teachers collect such contributions, suggest programs and speakers, help out in their own areas of special skill, write up the programs, and do myriad other "resourceful" things to build these valuable gifted programs.

"Half the school wants to be in it," the kids told me.

The teacher-counselor helps the students plan their own curriculums, and these plans vary widely. So far, in the junior high area especially, all that can be conceded by the powers-that-be is a slightly modified program of regular classes. But advanced or honors classes are usually available, and in fact are prescribed if the school is to receive state funds for the identified gifted students. The counselors may arrange for them to have one or two free periods to spend in the library, in their study-room, on a special field trip, or in other "enriching" ways such as the Sunshine School program at Hale Junior High, where students teach retarded children instead of just going on to study hall.

Another of the more common but limited plans is to have two "back-to-back" periods of English and social studies with a master-teacher who can also get his students released from other classes, so that they can take care of the work. There are worth-while activities their special teacher can supervise, such as the trip to the tidepools, a court trial, Student Congress meeting or a speech tournament. Exceptional teaching ability is needed in this plan.

Another plan used in O'Farrell Junior High is to gather the gifted students in a homeroom, and let them take as many different classes as they can handle by having them attend each one only two or three times a week, but requiring them to keep up with the class work. In fact, these kids not only keep pace but do extra reports! As William Vassar says, you have to overcome the resistance of teachers to this idea.

At the "left" end of the spectrum is the self-contained group of gifted students for whom "no bells toll." Much of their work is self-initiated; they may build units around their special interests, and the master teacher can guide them in directions that will encompass most of the skills they would ordinarily get in a regular English, history, science, or math class. This means the master teachers are also counselors.

High school students like these are sometimes released to take college classes on local campuses, or as elementary pupils they may visit junior high schools. Obviously this is going to lead to acceleration—or could we call it *exhilaration*? They learn because they want to learn, because they are free to learn.

Such programs are so new that not much has been written about "independent study" except in a very general way. A good chapter on the subject is to be found in *The Junior High and Middle Schools*, by Alvin W. Howard and George C. Stoumbis. Among the schools these authors discuss briefly are ungraded Melbourne High School in

Florida (for qualifying students); a New York school, grades 7-12 (any interested student may apply); a Pennsylvania school with grades 9 and 10 in which 97 percent of the student body was involved (see "Independent Study—For *All* Students" in *Phi Delta Kappan*, 47 [March 1966] Allan J. Glatthorn and J. F. Ferderbar); Winnetka, Illinois, Junior High School; and Theodore, Alabama, High School, grades 7-12.

One of the most exciting things about gifted education right now is the way the different states are sending representatives to observe each other's programs. In one month, in San Diego, I met consultants who had flown in from Missouri, Illinois, and Connecticut as well as from other parts of California, and a combined convention of CAG, NAG, and TAG was held in Long Beach in February 1972. These playful nicknames stand for California Association for Gifted Children, the National Association for Gifted Children, and The Association for Gifted, a division of the National Council for Exceptional Children. The National Association for Gifted Children held its last conference in Houston in October 1978. Their next general meeting is to be in Baltimore, Maryland in October of 1979. The California Association for the Gifted holds its annual conference in February. The site alternates between San Francisco, Los Angeles, and San Diego.

The World Council for Gifted and Talented Children was established in 1975 during the first World Conference held in London under the auspices of the National Association for Gifted Children (U.K.) A second World Conference was held in San Francisco in 1977 and the third in July in Jerusalem in 1979.

Seattle, Washington, Montclair, New Jersey, and Houston, Texas all have what is termed Magnate programs. These are schools or parts of school buildings that are set up so as to be available to qualifying children from all over town. Special programs for the gifted or near-gifted are provided within this set-up.

Programs for the gifted are bound to differ, to evolve from the needs of individual students, and probably to change from year to year. The outstanding Illinois Plan is based on this premise: "participating school districts are urged to develop programs that are as innovative and diverse as the talents of their students." The state provides consultants, materials, in-service training, and funds; in order to qualify for these, the individual school presents its plan of individualization, independent study, or curricular modification. Nothing could be more appropriate, since administrators, teachers, students and their talents, facilities of the school, and community resources and attitudes vary so widely not only from state to state, but from town to town.

Nothing in the field of education can be more *in*appropriate than refusing to let children learn as much as they can. They can't learn as much as they are capable of in districts that continue to let adult prejudices stemming from the 1920s and 1940s hold them back with slogans continually proven invalid, but which are still used to prevent today's children from learning as fast as they can. The resultant waste of time, effort, and money, and the boredom and frustration of both pupils and teachers, is incalculable.

As most schools are still set up in the traditional graded pattern, it seems advisable to accelerate gifted children in the elementary years (K-6) or in junior high. My earlier suggestion that we might abolish junior high was one of those brainstorms creative people get that are sure to shock the general populace, but nonetheless seventh and eighth grades do provide little other than review of elementary subjects and an orientation toward senior high. There are notable exceptions to this generalization, of course, but not enough exceptions to change my point of view.

"In seventh and eighth grades I felt kinda useless," a gifted student said. "I was only drifting."

Responsible educators like Ruth Strang ("a good plan seems to be to complete the first three grades in two years and the three junior high grades in two years") support the thesis that valuable time can be saved for good students in the early grades, when they learn the basics faster than average-ability children do, and have to sit around a lot. If they are not allowed to move ahead after learning the basics, they would miss later opportunities to cover more areas of learning. When they finally graduate from junior high to high school—with its wide choice of major academic subjects needed for college, variety of languages, typing, art, music, drama and other electives, vocational exploratory courses, and a wealth of extracurricular activities—at a time when social life is more important to the kids than ever before, they don't begin to have time for it all.

Current suggestions for the gifted in high school include Dr. James Bryant Conant's (1966) "give them more work:" as a minimum, four years of math, four years of foreign language, three years of science, four years of English and three of social studies, and advanced placement college level courses. He also suggests shortening periods so they could take art or music as well as five solids and the required physical education and driver's ed. At the opposite pole is a Los Angeles recommendation (1972) that academic subject requirements be cut and even students planning on college and professional careers — all students — be required to prepare for a trade before they could receive a high school diploma. Financial constraints currently being imposed on many school districts may not make a variety of electives possible.

Vocational education is certainly a good thing, and we should have more of it (only more realistic options for *today's* job market), but for gifted students this is ridiculous! And the work involved in Dr. Conant's stringent academic requirements might not be too much if implemented in some sort of flexible scheduling or independent-study plan, but in the traditional fifty-minute periods with lessons geared to the average mentality there would be too much wasted time just sitting in the classroom.

If elementary and junior high schools would offer additional courses (as some do) for gifted children to take in their spare time (such as more than "token" science, typing, several languages, and algebra in junior high), then acceleration at this level would not be so necessary. Then when gifted boys and girls get to high school they wouldn't have to "give up" typing, speech, or a second language. Also, the current emphasis on acceleration in high school *rather than* in the earlier grades would make more sense.

Currently, all major private universities in the country and many state universities offer advanced placement or credit for high school students who score three's, four's, or five's on the College Entrance Examination Boards Advanced Placement examinations. As a result, much student time and tuition fees are saved when some of our brightest students are granted admission to colleges and universities with sophomore standing.

Leta Hollingworth, too, said the gifted in elementary schools are wasting their time. Studies over a three-year period showed that one-quarter of all children could master all the mental work in half the time, while children of 170 IQ could do all the studies with top marks in about one-fourth of the time they are "compelled" to spend in school.

"They teach themselves to read backwards," she said, "just to fill up the hours."

But, as Jean Piaget says, "the results of a teaching method are much more closely tested and checked when it is destined for use on adults, who have no time to waste . . . than in the case of children, for whom time spent in study is just as precious in fact, but does not appear so in many people's eyes."

A word of caution lest the issue of providing enrichment or acceleration for gifted kids be thought simple. No plan to accommodate their needs is any better than the care and thought that goes into that plan. Capricious planning results in less than optimum results!

SPECIAL INTEREST REFERENCES:

Gallagher, James. *Teaching the Gifted Child*. Boston: Allyn & Bacon, 1975. This is the best single volume on issues relating to education of the gifted. His chapters on enrichment in the various subject areas can provide much guidance to parents and teachers.

Correspondence with the College Entrance Examination Board, Princeton, New Jersey, 08540 will yield information regarding the nature of the national Advanced Placement Program.

Fifth and sixth graders hold a seminar at Pacific tide pools. (Photo courtesy of San Diego School District)

Eugene W. Stark as a 16-year-old junior at Johns Hopkins University converses with Dr. Julian C. Stanley, Professor of Psychology and Director of the Study of Mathematically Precocious Youth (SMPY) there. (Photo courtesy of Dr. Julian Stanley)

At Talcott Mountain Science Center in Connecticut, students are shown how to use an optical theodolite to trace weather balloons and determine speed of winds aloft. (Photo courtesy of Dr. William Vassar)

Mark Hodes, Palo Alto mathematics teacher, teaches especially able elementary school mathematicians the principle of diminishing returns. (Photo courtesy of Lucille M. Nixon School)

9
What Makes a "Gifted" Teacher?
Who Should Teach the Gifted?

Issues:
  Should a teacher of the gifted be gifted?
  What characteristics in a teacher do gifted students prize most highly?
  How is a teacher of the gifted different from a "regular" teacher?
  What has more value—learning facts or learning how to learn?

JOHN DRYDEN (17th-century English poet and satirist): *Genius must be born, and never can be taught.*

CARL LINNAEUS (18th-century Swedish professor and botanist): *A professor can never better distinguish himself than by encouraging a clever pupil, for the true discoverers are among them, as the comets among the stars.*

GOETHE (German poet and philosopher, 1749-1832): *A teacher who can arouse a feeling for one good action, for one single good poem, accomplishes more than he who fills our memory with rows on rows of natural objects, classified with name and form.*

HENRY ADAMS (writer, editor, historian, in *The Education of Henry Adams*, 1907): *What one knows is, in youth, of little moment; they know enough who know how to learn.*

ROBERT F. DEHAAN (1963): *The teacher's task is more a matter of directing learning, providing materials, and making suggestions to youngsters who are eager and capable of learning rapidly.*

JOHN HOLT (1967): *I would be against trying to cram knowledge into the heads of children, even if we could agree on what knowledge to cram, and could be sure that it would not go out of date, even if we could be sure that, once crammed in, it would stay in. For it seems to me a fact that . . . in our struggle to make sense out of life, the things we most need to learn are the things we most want to learn. . . . We want to know for a reason.*

NEIL POSTMAN AND CHARLES WEINGARTNER (1969): *The only way to learn where a kid is "at" is to listen to what he is saying.*

BENJAMIN DE MOTT (in a review of James Herndon's *How to Survive in our Native Land*, *Saturday Review*, September 18, 1971): [*Herndon*] *knows that smart, hardworking, imaginative, decent kids can still, on occasion, be a serious pain in the tail for smart, hardworking imaginative, decent teachers.*

FIFTH GRADER (1975): *Teach us to learn and then step aside so that we can learn.*

JOHN CURTIS GOWAN AND CATHERINE BRUCH (in "What Makes a Creative Person a Creative Teacher?" *The Gifted Child Quarterly*, Vol. 11, 1967): *The teacher needs a great deal of energy, self-confident daring, a warm outgoing nature . . . and besides being intelligent and original the teacher must be free of hasty, impatient behavior on the one hand and of anal authoritarianism on the other. With such an order it is not surprising we have so much trouble in getting creative behavior in students.*

SIDNEY P. MARLAND, JR. (1971): *Studies of successful teachers for the gifted typically have dealt with their characteristics and behavior more often than with their specific preparation. In general, the successful teachers are highly intelligent, are interested in scholarly and artistic pursuits, have wide interests, are mature and unthreatened, possess a sense of humor, are more student centered than their colleagues, and are enthusiastic about both teaching and advanced study for themselves.*

GILBERT HIGHET (Professor and writer, classicist, 1954): *Real teaching is not simply handing out packages of information. It culminates in a conversion, an actual change of the pupil's mind.*

ALVIN EURICH (1969): . . . *the American creative genius must concentrate on making the best possible use of the most gifted teachers now at work or that can be recruited and trained.* As Fortune *magazine has said: "There never can be enough truly gifted teachers; the qualities that make for greatness in teaching—like those that make for greatness in any field—are rare."*

JEAN PIAGET (1969, commenting on an experiment in the Malting House School in Cambridge, England, where children of 3-8 were given a laboratory to experiment in all by themselves): *Some form of systematization applied by the adult would perhaps not have been wholly harmful to the pupils. . . . As for those new methods of education that have had the most durable success, and which without doubt constitute the foundation of tomorrow's active school, they all more or less draw their inspiration from a golden mean. [There is] necessity . . . for a surrounding social structure entailing not merely cooperation among the children but also cooperation with adults.*

The paradox here is that there is little doubt as to what makes a good teacher; yet many go right on teaching in the same poor ways.

The controversy is unspoken and unprinted.

Men like James Herndon and Jonathan Kozol teach the children instead of the facts—and get fired (coast to coast, from San Francisco to Boston). Enthusiastic young (and old) teachers try out new ideas, and parents complain.

The children rarely complain! Many of them in innovative programs are enjoying school for the first time in their lives—and learning how to learn. It is the parents who don't know what is going on (the ones who don't even take the trouble to find out), and the administrators (who don't like to listen to the vocal minority of parents) who are too set in their ways to fight for the necessary revolution in education.

Charles Silberman reports on the need for change in his massive best-seller, *Crisis in the Classroom*, and he is talking about all children. In over 500 pages he barely mentions the gifted as having any special needs.

Outstanding teachers like John Holt don't either; the truth is that if teachers and schools all could be like the ideal that educational philosophers are advocating today, we might not need any special groups or classes or schools for our best students, because the ideal is an individualized education for each child.

No one can quarrel with this philosophy; the only trouble is, we are a long way from putting it into practice, and we need the gifted children of this generation to put it into practice in the next.

The 1960s are called the Education Decade. Actually, good new ideas as well as a revived interest in gifted children have been exploding since the 1950s, with Paul Witty's classic, *The Gifted Child*, published in 1951 after a long period of educational doldrums. When I went to college in the late 1930s we took education courses because we had to, in order to get teaching jobs. Back in graduate school in 1969, after raising my family, I had to take another course, in curriculum, to complete my California State teaching credential, and I groaned at the thought.

The textbook, lectures, and true-false, multiple-choice exams were still dull; the teaching method had changed very little in thirty years, but oddly enough, the *content* made more sense. My professor recommended *Education and Ecstasy*, just out that year, and articles in education and general magazines like the *Phi Delta Kappan*, *Changing Times*, *Look* and the *Saturday Review*. I didn't share his enthusiasm until I began to read them—they were interesting!

They all said we shouldn't teach by the memorize-and-regurgitate method that some of my college professors and most of my grandchildren's grade-school teachers are still using. I asked my education professor why, since he obviously enjoyed the new ideas, he still gave us those exams from a textbook, and marked us wrong if we didn't say exactly what the book said, word for word.

He *didn't* say, "You're right! I won't do that anymore." And he went on giving the tests.

The trouble remains that the good ideas are still theories rarely used in our schools, and the general public, including many teachers, have scarcely heard of them. The top priority in needs uncovered by the recent Department of Health, Education and Welfare's investigation of the state of education for the gifted and talented was for "better prepared teachers."

Most (though not all) authorities agree that gifted children, because of their unusual abilities or special skills, need a different kind of teaching and different kinds of teachers; advanced states like

Illinois and Connecticut and California have already begun to educate teachers in the special field of gifted education, either before or during their service as teachers.

The Office of Education suggests teaching fellowships and in-service training as major needs to "better prepare" these teachers; Professor Gowan pointed out in *Educating the Ablest* (in 1971) that only the University of Georgia, Penn State, Kent State, George Peabody College, the University of Illinois, and the University of Connecticut were prepared to give graduate degrees in gifted educa-tion. At this writing, additional colleges, including San Diego State University, are preparing teachers for gifted children. The state of California now offers a credential in education of the gifted. The State Universities of Dominguez Hills, Los Angeles, Fresno, and Northridge, offer courses leading to a Masters degree. Dr. Barbara Clark of California State University, Los Angeles, has been in-strumental in this State University movement.

As a first step for improving administrative personnel, the federal government made available $200,000 for a Leadership Training In-stitute in Chicago in the summer of 1972. Dr. David Jackson of Il-linois, Director, was assisted by Irving Sato (California) and William Vassar (Connecticut).

The Leadership Training Institute, based in Los Angeles and under the directorship of Dr. Irving Sato, serves teachers and ad-ministrators throughout this country and in other parts of the world. A strong feature of the Institute is that outstanding teachers and ad-ministrators take part in their workshops and serve as "mentor models." Sandy Kaplan, Dick Sholseth, and Allyn Arnold, all of Los Angeles, and Bruce DeVries of Ukiah, California, have made signifi-cant contributions to teachers of the gifted through the Institute.

The enthusiasm of teachers who are teaching the gifted in special programs is a heartening development. Many of them spend their own time and money on courses to improve their ability to instruct gifted students.

These teachers band together in associations (with dues!) such as the Association of San Diego Educators for the Gifted, which represents 800 teachers of classes for gifted students. They attend workshops and conferences, visit good programs or instructional media centers, and cooperate with parent groups. The San Diego

Parents Association has one thousand members; others in California, like the San Fernando Valley association, have even more. And parents all over the country gave valuable help in the regional hearings conducted by the Department of Health, Education and Welfare for the Report to Congress.

Mrs. Ruth Fenton of the Monterey Peninsula in California, and Chairperson of the Parent Committee of the California Association for Gifted organization, is a dedicated, hard-working advocate for the gifted and is mobilizing parents and professionals to effect legislative action on behalf of gifted children.

The rapport between parents and teachers is getting better every day, especially where there are special programs for gifted and talented children (not that there aren't some cases of emotionally disturbed parents!). But in communities where innovations are frowned on parents and teachers are still ancient and honorable enemies, and the kids are the ones who suffer.

I was invited to visit a gifted group: 67 sixth-graders, about one-third of them identified-gifted. For over an hour the children asked the most intimate and searching questions about my book, *Johnny*, which they all had read. They asked about life and death and illness and family relations and writing books, and I answered simply and honestly to the most attentive audience I have ever experienced.

We were talking about courage and sense of humor — they laughed hilariously at Johnny's corniest jokes — when one boy asked seriously, "Did he ever get depressed?"

I knew my answer *mattered* to that boy, though I didn't know why. "Yes, sure," I said. "But he never stayed depressed very long."

"He seems like a pretty neat guy," he said. "I'd like him for a friend."

I came away with the overwhelming conviction that with children like these, we don't have to worry about the future.

Some of the special characteristics teachers of these children should ideally have are discussed by the authorities at the beginning of this chapter. Gowan and Torrance's up-to-date book of readings, *Educating the Ablest*, 1979, is helpful on this and other subjects, as is Gallagher's *Teaching Gifted Students*, 1975. Also, Ruth Martinson's book on curriculum enrichment contains a thoughtful section on the teacher of the gifted.

Choosing teachers who are suited to conduct programs for gifted is challenging. When some students were asked in a study completed not long ago, "With what kind of teacher do you learn best, most enjoyably, and in depth?" responses included: ". . . a teacher that lets you do independent work" . . . "a teacher who lets you work at your own speed" . . . "a teacher who gives you choice—I like to discover facts and things rather than having someone tell me" . . . "I like a teacher who does not help you all the time, only when you really need it" . . . "a teacher who acts like he really cares for you and makes things fun for the whole class" . . . "one who doesn't interrupt and change the subject" . . . "a teacher who takes suggestions" . . . "a teacher who is humorous and playful in his approach to instruction."

Gifted children can be difficult for regular teachers. On October 31, 1975, Charles McCabe, popular columnist in the San Francisco *Chronicle*, spoke of the traits of the gifted child:

> Gifted kids are "high spirited" if you like them, "emotionally unstable" if you don't. If he lets his feelings rip, the gifted child is urged by his teacher to pipe down or more commonly nowadays he is placed on a regimen of ritalin or some other kind of drug which, among other bad effects, interferes with the play of his feelings which is the gifted child's capital. This kind of child can be told two things: that he is showing independence and that he is admirable or that he is being rebellious and, therefore, bad. There is nothing of malice in the gifted child's asserting of his highly individual self. When his independence is seen to be malicious, the fight for the gifted child and what he can offer society is just about lost.

Given a teacher with at least one of the qualifications most needed for teaching in this field—enthusiasm—what are the new, or newly recognized, ways of teaching that will make learning as exciting as it should be? For *all* children?

Few parents and community members who still insist that "what was good enough for me is good enough for the kids today" can also say they *liked* school; very few of the most outstanding men and women of the 20th century, discussed in *Cradles of Eminence*, felt that they learned much, if anything, in school.

The wonder is that so many have submitted so docilely for so long to the dullest method of teaching there is. Memorize and repeat, memorize and repeat. . . .

What about the "inquiry method"? It's a commonplace word now in innovative circles; no one bothers to explain it to the many parents, and even teachers, who don't know exactly how it works. Briefly, you don't *tell* the child, you ask him questions (or have him ask you questions) which lead him to learning for himself. When he learns this way, he *understands* and is more likely to *remember*. In the old lecture or even in the "discussion" method, the teacher directed the thoughts of every child (typically, *en bloc*).

But thoughts don't come that way, which brings us to more of the newly popular theories: teachers should encourage inductive reasoning and divergent rather than convergent thinking. Inductive reasoning starts where we used to leave off — give the child some facts, or tell him where to find them, and let him use them, think with them as material, formulate his own ideas, as highly creative and mentally gifted children can. As for "divergent thinking," this results in many different ideas, rather than the "one right answer" teachers have been demanding inexorably ever since *I* can remember.

The teacher-directed conclusion doesn't require any thinking at all, usually; it's just rote memory. Everybody who thinks about it admits rote memory isn't of much use since knowledge has been doubling every ten years — and as it increases, it often changes as well.

What did you get out of school?

(This is a little exercise in the inquiry method which is supposed to make you realize what I'm driving at without my telling you.)

Silence?

Teachers shouldn't be afraid of silence.

You probably came up with some scattered facts (red, yellow and blue are primary colors, Columbus discovered America, or was it the Vikings?) and dates (1066, 1492, 1776). You also came up with some learning skills: how to read, how to write, how to do research in a library, how to type, how to drive a car, or to use lab equipment for scientific experiments, or whatever you "took."

Which have you enjoyed or used the most? The facts or the skills?

Most people will agree that an education should teach us not so much facts as where to find them, and not descriptions or discussions of activities but how to *do* them. Why then do we keep on teaching children to recite facts? Why keep using up valuable skill-teaching time to test students on the contents of a textbook which is either out of date or soon will be, or which, at best, they will forget?

If you're lucky enough to live in an innovative district where no one teaches like this anymore, sing hallelujah. San Diego is generally recognized as being in the forefront of educational reform, and yet a teacher's comment at the bottom of a *junior college* student's test last month read, "Your opinions are valuable. But, when we have an exam on the *textbook*, we're interested in what the *textbook* has to say — right?" (The student's opinion — on how a person feels before giving a speech! — was absolutely valid, but he got a B — instead of an A because he didn't give the textbook writer's feelings!)

If you are a parent, do you know how your children's teachers are teaching them? If you don't like it, what can you do about it?

Maybe you have the answer. I don't know. (A constantly mentioned attribute of a good teacher for the gifted is the nerve to admit that.) Of course, you can always write your Congressmen. That's what sparked the 1971 investigation that disclosed the nationwide neglect of the gifted.

If you are a teacher, and your principal says that you have to "cover" a textbook, give tests, make out report cards, and keep the kids quiet all the time, what can you do? Only the great teachers have any answers, but creative men and women all over the United States, in the old schools against opposition and in the modern schools with support, *are trying*. Some of them are succeeding.

Community persons can be highly effective teachers of the gifted. Many districts have Regional Occupation Programs that assign students to various businesses, industries, hospitals, and schools, in order to provide them with insights into occupations and to make learning a part of the whole life scene rather than one confined within the walls of a school. One student assigned to a laboratory for infectious diseases concluded his experience with a research paper on the "Anti-Bacterial Defense System of the Lung." Another conducted research at Lockheed Space Industry that was presented to a national meeting of space scientists. A number of very gifted young people feel a commitment to helping children in Centers for the Retarded or working with children with other handicaps. School credit is given for these experiences. But the real credit goes to the tireless workers — school people — who round up the community volunteers, find new and exciting programs and who carefully match the student to the experience.

In another program, an independent-study student at Pt. Loma High describes a creative use of Pacific Telephone Company's *conference phone call* plan:

"Five of us studied anthropology and read all of Margaret Mead's books. Then our principal made arrangements for a conference phone call. We called her and held a seminar with her. She was in New York and we were in San Diego. Following this I got so excited that I read about the Palauan, Bunyoro, Tiwi, Gururumba, Kapauku, and many other societies."

A sophomore high school teacher forced to teach *Silas Marner* didn't just grumble at its irrelevance, as most teachers do; her students put out a newspaper about the town Silas lived in, with (historical) news, editorials, sports pages, letters-to-the-editor, lovelorn columns, and comics. They did the same thing with *Julius Caesar* and other "classic" assignments. Another teacher might think of something even better to do with Caesar—the point is to do *something* with it. Of course, it's a lot more work, but WORK is more fun than BLAH.

Another group of students used their spare time over and above the required subjects for their social studies laboratory; they furnished and took care of the lab room, gave special reports like "The Genesis of a Slum," using community resources. They also found a town-owned island in the Connecticut River that they proposed for use as a school wildlife center, and they put out a journal called *Contact*—about "what education can be." Note that in this case the teacher seems hardly necessary, and the term "faculty friend" could well be used as a model in all independent studies projects.

An especially talented teacher arranged a weekend "retreat" at a school camp for gifted students and some of their parents and teachers; over 120 were there. Imagine a meeting of so many bright young minds under the mountain live-oaks, the sun, and the stars—with classes in astronomy, Indian culture, creative dramatics, and comparative religion, along with "rap sessions" on ecology, war, discrimination, drugs, population, moral standards, law enforcement, books they had read, and the draft.

In the creative dramatics sessions, which I led, we came up—in less than an hour—with skits for the campfire, including a serious social drama as well as the funny ones we did in other groups.

After I explained how creative dramatics works (each character makes up his own dialog as he acts out the part), the kids worked out their plot—I just asked some good questions, like "What about a social problem we could use for a theme?"

They came up with "people who see someone getting beat up or robbed or even killed but refuse to get involved."

"Where should we set it?"

"A city street."

"Who would be there? What character would you like to be?"

"I'll be the murderer," said a girl!

Another girl said she'd be the one who was killed, a teacher said he'd be a policeman, three boys decided to be playing ball, somebody's mother offered to be a store-keeper. I asked for volunteers to be a married couple walking by, someone else said she'd be a "nosy neighbor" looking out a window, another a shopper in a hurry.

"What could be the motive for the murder?"

"She's on drugs!"

And so it evolved. The policeman walked by—too early and too late. The boys played ball and did nothing about the girl who was acting so strangely. The victim came out of the store and was attacked. No one helped her, then or later, as she lay dying. The married couple walked by and argued about it. By the time the policeman strolled by again, the girl was dead.

He questioned the boys playing ball, the lady in the window, the storekeeper. Nobody saw anything. Nobody got involved.

One of the young men who led a rap session on discrimination used the inquiry method in the extreme form advocated by Neil Postman and Gerald Weingartner. They suggest using only three teacher statements in a class period, otherwise all questions. More statements would subject the teacher to a fine of 25 cents each.

I would go broke!

Sometimes little comes out of a session like this, the leader told me afterwards, but other times the class explodes, and it's an unforgettable learning experience. One difficulty is that the teacher, in bending over backwards not to admit that there is only "one right answer," may simply pass on, without comment, to another child for another answer and leave the child who answered wondering if he is stupid.

This contradicts the strong recommendation of today's educators that children need a good "self-image." We could at least say, without it costing us 25 cents, "That's a good idea!" and *then* ask for others. Children do need praise.

There is a "golden mean," agrees Jean Piaget, who has far more influence in the field of education than I; and even Dr. Suchman, whose name is linked with the inquiry method, explains in the debate at the beginning of this chapter that statements (lecture, the didactic method) are sometimes more appropriate than questions.

We shouldn't waste the pupil's time in *not* teaching him anymore than we should waste it in the forced feeding of irrelevant facts. As a steady diet all questions could become just as boring as all answers.

Teachers in training shouldn't believe everything they hear, but on the other hand there are a lot of good ideas floating around these days, and the inquiry method is one of the best, if not carried to extremes.

As a smart seventh-grader told me the other day, her brown eyes twinkling, "You can't believe half what you read in the papers, so I'll believe the half *I* want to!"

If you want to be a good teacher, first, *be informed*, and then *be yourself*. That includes breaking out of the old molds, but it also means not confining yourself in any new ones. Your freedom to teach is as important to your students as their freedom to learn, and most authorities believe that divergent teaching styles are a good thing. The trouble is, that teachers haven't been free to teach.

And we've all been so frantically busy teaching the wrong way that we're only beginning to realize how much easier it is to teach — and to learn — in better ways.

If only we are allowed to.

There is hope. Even my education textbook, in 1969, concluded with, "It is the teachers who experiment in their classes who make the changes that really count. They should be encouraged to do so, for without this experimentation, curricula and courses become dreary." (Clark, Klein and Burks. *The American Secondary School Curriculum*. New York, Macmillan Company, 1964.)

But four years after the publication of this text, such a teacher, Dave Hermanson, conducting such an experiment (the Independent Studies program for gifted students offered at Pt. Loma High School in 1968), said in an interview for their school paper, "Changing the curricula is like moving a cemetery. The miscellaneous information, scattered and divided data, chaos and incoherence, one textbook, worksheets, Friday movie, Pavlov bell and the 55-minute learning module are so deeply entrenched in the godliness of order, neatness and silence that little change is likely to take place for quite a while."

Within four years, though, there were five of these Independent Studies centers in San Diego, and they have been commended by top national authorities like John Curtis Gowan and William Vassar. With the gifted as pioneers, perhaps some day all students can have this same freedom from the "Pavlov bell."

SPECIAL INTEREST REFERENCES:

There does not appear to be a current extended discussion of who should teach the gifted. The references cited in the body of this chapter are fine, but short. Paul Torrance has a chapter in *Gifted Children in the Classroom*, on "Becoming a Teacher of Gifted Children." Most references will, of course, contain implications for teaching. You will need to seek them out.

I might suggest Sylvia Aston Warner's *Teacher* (New York: Bantam, 1971), for a sensitive treatise on the nature of the general teaching task.

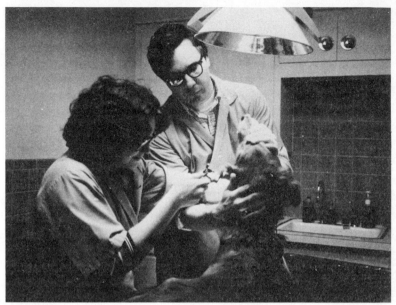

An intern works as a special assistant to her sponsor, a veterinarian, in the Executive High School Internship Program in Wichita, Kansas. (Photo courtesy of Shirlene R. Duncan)

Students at the Pennsylvania Governor's School for the Arts are videotaping what music looks like. Using a video tape recorder and camera, they are filming the image on the oscilloscope produced by the sound of the synthesizer. (Photos courtesy of Pennsylvania Governor's School for the Arts.)

Four student filmmakers worked with two professionals to make a new 16mm. color synchronized-sound film for the Pennsylvania Governor's School for the Arts.

A music major at the Pennsylvania Governor's School for the Arts plays the harp.

Pennsylvania Governor's School for the Arts students study leadership to help them promote the arts in their home schools and communities. Here, a student presents a program she has developed.

10
What Can Parents Do?
What Is Parent Power?

Issues:
What does an IQ in the gifted range mean?
How should parents respond to the information that their child is gifted?
What should parents do to stimulate the intellectual development of their gifted child?
What is the difference between pushing and stimulating?
What can parents do to encourage school programs for gifted students?

JOHN CURTIS GOWAN AND GEORGE DEMOS (1964): *The question sometimes arises as to whether parents should be told that their child is gifted. . . . Should parents be told their son has made the varsity football squad? Should they be told he has been elected Class President? . . . Should they be told he plans to go to college? The answer to all these questions is "Yes."*

LOUISE BATES AMES (1967): *If parents could think more of a high IQ as a good thing to have and less as a measure of the child's total functioning, they would be less likely to fall into the trap of pushing their children ahead in school . . . just because they are bright.*

JOHN CURTIS GOWAN (in "Twenty-Five Suggestions for Parents of Able Children," *Gifted Child Quarterly,* Vol. 8, 1964): *There's a difference between pushing and intellectual stimulation. Parents should avoid "pushing" a child into reading, "exhibiting" him before others or courting undue publicity about him. On the other hand, parents should seek in every way to stimulate and widen the child's mind, through suitable experiences in books, recreation, travel, and the arts.*

A community opinion on MIKE GROST, who later graduated from the University of Michigan, with honors, at 14): *So you're little Mike Grost? Your parents like to think you're a genius, huh?*

MIKE GROST: *No, sir. My parents prefer to think of me as a natural resource.* [This anecdote is taken from Audrey Grost's *Genius in Residence*, 1970.]

JAMES GALLAGHER (1959): *Gifted children are among our most important national resources. . . .[but] How often have you heard the following statement from parents? "Well, my Johnny is not a genius, but at least he is all right in the head."*

RUTH STRANG (1960): *Gifted children vary so widely. . . . Some need control; others need freedom. Some are overstimulated; others need to be challenged. . . . Some receive an embarrassing amount of praise and recognition; others need more outspoken appreciation.*

PAUL D. PLOWMAN AND JOSEPH P. RICE (California State Consultants in gifted education, 1969): . . . *"Successful programs" are abandoned because they are exposed to incessant pressure from teachers and parents. . . . There is clearly a need to study the social, cultural, and psychological motives of parents and teachers rejecting programs that involve unconventional approaches, risk-taking, or unusual commitment.*

WILLARD ABRAHAM (1958): *For too long parents and teachers have been wary of each other, worried that the other will stand in judgment, find fault, and lack understanding. When it comes to the gifted, or any other child, neither is a* better *judge; the observation, knowledge, and cooperation of both is needed.*

An elementary school teacher in an individualized program using parents as teachers' aides (1978): *We couldn't do it without the parents.*

So you have a healthy child.

Lucky you!

So you have a gifted child.

Lucky you!

Lucky you, not because you can now point to your child as an extension of yourself (if he's gifted, I must be too), but rather because your child has the potential for achieving success in academic pursuits. His success then lends itself to feelings of self-worth and provides the confidence needed to tackle tasks which have the appearance of great difficulty. Success and confidence make it safe to take risks. The possibility of failure does not diminish the excitement and enthusiasm engendered by a challenge. So, lucky you. Lucky child.

Ruth Strang in *Helping Your Gifted Child* says, "It takes four things to make a gifted child: a good heredity, favorable experiences in infancy and childhood, an environment that offers opportunities for the development of abilities, and guidance and instruction." She further states that, "From their parents, gifted children need acceptance without exploitation, understanding without prejudice and guidance without domination."

All of that is a lot to think about, but it translates into some fairly simple action.

Do not expect the child to be equally good at all things. Be patient while he learns the things that are harder for him. A gifted older brother in my acquaintance depended on a less gifted sister to tie his shoes for him until he was seven. A highly gifted high school student needed the patience of a good friend to learn to ride a bicycle.

Do not fall into the Madison Avenue Trap. In spite of what they (Madison Avenue) say, loving and caring cannot be equated with stuff—material possessions. The poor do indeed have equal opportunity to provide for their children in the loving and caring department. As a matter of fact, some of our most affluent children are among our most deprived. A new bicycle, the newest games, or a high-fi set are no substitute for parents' time. To spend time with a child says, "You're important. I'm giving you part of my life."

The value of simple playthings cannot be overestimated. Cans from the kitchen cupboard make great building blocks (also serve as early reading texts); cardboard cartons used by active young minds become trains, castles, space ships, or cocoons. Do you remember how you learned to make wise decisions? Did you ever make a mistake? Did you learn from that mistake? Making good decisions is a skill that requires practice. Let your child practice. He becomes a better ball player by practicing; so will he become a better decision-maker.

There is no substitute for time spent on this earth. Therefore, to expect more of a child than he can deliver is unfair. In many ways a gifted child is no older than the time he has been around—a gifted six-year-old is still just a six-year-old developmentally and emotionally. A gifted adolescent must go through many of the same developmental stages as do his less gifted friends and brothers and sisters.

Many of the gifted children in Victor and Mildred Goertzel's book, *Cradles of Eminence*, suffered a great deal of unhappiness, and if that is the price, do we want to pay it? Perhaps that is why the children in the ghetto may be the eminent men and women of tomorrow; perhaps pain is a prerequisite for production. But if we can, we as parents certainly want to raise *happily* gifted children.

I can't speak from experience as far as genius is concerned, but I have picked up a few ideas from raising a moderately gifted family; they may be of some help to those of you who are just beginning, or of nostalgic interest to others whose sons and daughters are growing or grown up. Also, I've talked to some parents of the highly gifted for their experiences.

Soon after our first daughter, Frea, was born, I learned Rule One (in order, not in importance): don't brag about your child, or you will be very unpopular with other parents. I have to admit I did not follow this rule without numerous exceptions for the next twenty years while I raised four lovely, beautiful, bright, delightful daughters and sons, but anyway I *knew* better.

"Give Mom an opening and she'll plunge right in," a teenage son once said in mingled disgust, resignation, and tender indulgence.

I did, however, develop an antidote; I made it a point to say the nicest things I could think of about other people's children too. This is easy, because I like children.

There is a sort of parents'-eye-view that makes it easier to see the virtues *and* faults in your own children than in others. When Frea was a baby I thought she had the most beautiful dimpled knees in the world, and I had a neighbor whose baby's legs looked like toothpicks. Of course I never *said* this, I just thought it. What I said was, "Sally's hair is so pretty. I wish Frea had curly hair. But I *do* like her legs."

"Oh, do you?" my neighbor sniffed. "They're so fat!"

The next rule I remember learning was when my second daughter was in the second grade. She had skipped the first because Frea, two years older, in playing school with her, had inconsiderately taught her how to read before the first grade teacher had a chance.

Sheila Mary was a chubby little girl; when she sang "I'm a little teapot, short and stout," she looked the part, and we thought she was adorable. But she came home from school one day with a smile that even her parents had to admit was a bit smug.

"Why did I skip a grade, Mother? Am I *very smart?*" she asked.

I reached fast for Rule Two: teach your little ones not to brag about themselves, or they will very unpopular with other children. "Yes, honey," I said, "but you were just lucky you were born that way—it's what you do with it that counts. Don't go around bragging about it, though, or you won't have any friends."

Since she was the most socially conscious child in our family anyway, I never had to say any more. In fact, I've wondered since if I should have laid it on so thick, because this leads up to Rule Three, which is probably the most important. As parents (particularly of *highly* gifted children) *you must not be too concerned about what other people think, and you must help your child to cope with the way people think.*

If this seems to be a contradiction, I don't mean it to be. The first two rules apply on *unimportant* occasions, and by following them you make it easier for your children to live in a society where they are in the minority. Besides the mentally gifted, this includes the highly creative or talented children with lower intelligence quotients who are frequently the children with the greatest potential for outstanding accomplishments—if their originality is not discouraged by conventional friends and neighbors, or extinguished in a traditional school.

Charlotte Malone, Director, Educational Programs, University of California at San Diego, warns that parents too often object to special gifts like art or music as a "waste of time," and want their children to "get ahead" in some "practical" field.

On the other hand, a mother of a gifted child at a panel of parents I attended recently wanted to know if she should insist on piano lessons. Don't choose an "art" for them either, but do, as she did, provide the opportunity (a piano) if you can.

It should be obvious that we can't expect average behavior from children who are not average, and it would be a shame to let them succumb to group pressure and become just like everybody else if we can't start them off in early childhood with the intellectual courage to be themselves. It would be stupid — and cruel — to try to force such children into molds cut to a size that is too small for them. Yet that is what is being done by many well-meaning educators and parents all over the country. Such people think the children "will be happier," but they omit the fact that *learning* is one of the greatest pleasures of life, and the more one is capable of learning the happier it makes one.

The admonition not to brag is an example of a less important matter. Actually, boasting is not a common characteristic of gifted children. Terman's and other studies have shown that the gifted have an inborn humility; as Socrates believed, the truly wise know that they don't know. Bright children are less apt to be boastful than the average, since they have more reason to have confidence in themselves and don't need to bolster it up (at least in the intellectual area). They do *need* that confidence, however, if they are going to put their marvelous ideas into practice (like Benjamin Franklin's kite, for example). So people, especially teachers, who try to "take them down a peg," are discouraging the artists, explorers, and inventors of the future.

As parents, my husband, and I may have made a mistake when our fifteen-year-old son was No. 2 in U.S. Boys' Tennis (a sport we recommend highly for gifted children especially). One day when he was about to play another good player, we overheard David say, disgustedly, "I couldn't lose to *him*."

Since our son had always been a nice boy we wanted him to stay that way, so we lit into him. He took it to heart, and in the next tournament he lost to that boy for the first time. The question seems to be whether you want to raise a champion athlete or a modest person; it does take a great deal of confidence to be No. 1 in the world at anything. It is possible of course to be a champion who has both confidence and compassion — but it's difficult.

However it was David's own choice that, after college when he was very near the top, he gave up tournament tennis to become a Ph.D., a teacher of medieval history, and an idealistic family man.

This brings up another rule; parents have no business making a choice of vocation for any child. Children often do follow in their father's footsteps, but all you can do is exemplify a worthwhile and satisfying career — as my husband, a college English professor, in fact did. Johnny too wanted to teach — math.

The other day I met a father, a successful black educator, who was very concerned about his son, who had an IQ based on the Binet test, at age ten, of almost 180. But the boy had not, he felt, fulfilled his promise. He had finished high school and gone to college, but then dropped out.

"I don't know where he is now," the father said, and I could sense his unspoken disappointment. "He's not doing anything just traveling around."

"How old is he?" I asked.

"He's twenty."

I couldn't tell him what is going to happen to his son, but I do know that twenty is the age for boys to wander through the world. At about seventeen, the year his boy went to college, they get a sudden surge of independence from parents and other adults. This is true of all boys but especially of the gifted. They are thinking things through, discarding the outmoded conventions and unthinking maxims and hypocrisies too many of us live by. They often rebel in college, become "radicals," lose their "religion," even if they were formerly orthodox Jews or devout Catholics. But a few years later when they have sown the traditional "wild oats" they usually become more conservative as they mature. I have seen them, boys and some girls too, return, like the Prodigal Son or Peer Gynt, to the home, to the church, to society.

"Everyone has a mass of bad work in him which he will have to work off and get rid of before he can do better," Samuel Butler wrote in *The Way of All Flesh*, "and indeed, the more lasting a man's ultimate good work, the more sure he is to pass through a time, and perhaps a very long one, in which there seems to be very little hope for him at all. We must all sow our spiritual wild oats."

Butler himself was the son of a minister who sent him to Cambridge to prepare for the ministry. But he went to New Zealand and worked on a sheep ranch! After he came back to England he composed music, painted pictures that were exhibited in the Royal Academy, and wrote a novel about a utopian land where there is no machinery (Erewhon, which is an anagram of nowhere). Later he wrote the even more famous *Way of All Flesh*.

I told this father about Samuel Butler, and added, "You mustn't expect your son to be like everybody else. He's one in a million."

He said, "You know, my son wanted to go to Australia and work on a sheep ranch !"

I can sympathize. It must be even harder for a minority father with an exceptionally gifted son just to "let him be."

Which brings us to another suggestion.

This will be an answer to these questions: How do you "discipline" a gifted child? Should you refrain? How permissive should you be? It makes sense to say that the parents of a young man or woman of twenty who has exceptional mental ability or talent—often, though not necessarily, much greater than their own—must expect him to make his own decisions.

But there was a time in the lives of these gifted sons and daughters when you were smarter than they were! When a child of exactly five years has an IQ of 150, which he will probably have within ten or fifteen points as he grows older, he is one in a thousand children, but he has what is called a "mental age" of seven years and four months. So you still have quite a few things to teach this child, *and you should.* Undisciplined creativity usually results in nothing getting done (a lazy Sir Isaac Newton could have seen the apple fall, had an idea—and done nothing about it); also, undisciplined genius may turn to evil instead of to good.

In one of Pearl Buck's novels of pre-revolution China, *Imperial Woman*, the young Empress was being admonished by her teacher. "You will inquire why I [teach you so.] I want you to learn precision and delicacy. You have power. But power must be informed and controlled from within. Then only may it be genius."

The probabilities indicate that when this same child is twelve years old with an IQ of 150 he will have a mental age of nineteen, which is considerably higher than the mental age of average adults. By this time, if you, his parents, are not especially gifted yourselves, you will have become increasingly aware that your child knows more than you do, at least in the "cognitive" (knowledge) area. But remember that a parent of average or even below-average mental ability may still have more to offer in the "affective" realm of feeling, and of values. The same rules apply to all parents of all children, no matter what their respective IQs: from earliest childhood on, give your children plenty of love, praise, and respect, and give them an increasing amount of responsibility and independence each year up to a mature (but these days maturity comes early) adulthood.

It's important for all parents, but especially for parents of the gifted who will be leaders in our society, to exemplify and teach a set of values, which the mentally gifted will understand even better than the average child. This must be done well before the age of six. "A child's character is largely formed by the age of six," psychologists have been telling us for years; the gifted child's character *may* largely be formed by the age of four, since his mental age may be six at that time.

A three-year-old of ours came to me one day with a very red face. "Would it be all right if I took a nickel out of your pocketbook?" she asked in a scared voice.

I swallowed a chuckle (they are so cute). "Oh, *no,* honey." I said solemnly. "That would be *stealing.*"

"Well," she gulped, and her face got even redder, "I already did."

After a moment of stern deliberation, while she quaked, I told her it was good of her to tell me, and that she should go and put it back. She did, with great relief, and from that day on my purse was as safe as a safe—with her. My other children went through similar incidents; most children do. That is how they learn.

When Johnny and a little pal stole some crackerjacks at the corner grocery at the age of five or six (the friendly grocer thought I ought to know) and Johnny *wouldn't* admit it, I spanked him. (This must be what educators mean by anal authoritarianism!)

"That hurt," he said piteously.

"It was meant to," I agreed.

"Well, I'm not used to it," he told me.

But it made the necessary impression. He didn't steal, and I can not honestly remember his telling lies anymore.

They do not learn if parents do not consider honesty at an early age important.

I have always thought it one of the most important of all values, and it has to be 100 percent, which one can not expect with most virtues. Jane Addams' father, one of the better parents in *Cradles of Eminence*, told her that mental integrity comes before everything else. And when you teach your children to be honest, not only with money but with words, you are also encouraging their originality, which is essential to creativity. Too many parents discourage honest statements in favor of what is conventional, and this is like destroying a child's gifts.

This does not mean courtesy and kindness are not just as important. It is not necessary to go around hurting people's feelings; we can always keep our mouths shut.

If you love your children, you want them to be good and to be happy; the two go together at least as far as any permanent well-being is concerned. You can not just let them do anything they want to do (like taking drugs "for kicks"); they don't even *want* you to let them do anything they want to, as many child psychologists have pointed out.

"Mother, can I wear high heels?" Sheila Mary asked me in the seventh grade. (Now there's a problem you won't encounter today!)

"No," I said, expecting the usual argument.

"Good," she said.

The type of discipline is not important as long as you persist in it as long as it is needed, and do it *because you love them*, because you care what kind of a character they have. You do whatever works with that particular child at that particular moment, but you have to be continually ingenious because all children are different—I used different methods with four children in the same family. But it was always based on the golden mean—not too permissive, not too strict.

You have to keep asking yourself which are the real values, and which the false, or conventional ones. The younger generation today makes a good point when they rebel at hypocrisies such as false modesty (prudery), false patriotism (chauvinism), or a hollow education. There are also some much less important "virtues" that the mother of a highly creative child, particularly, may have to dispense with. One of these is "neatness."

Creative children need *things* to create with; the highly regarded English "Infant Schools" call them *stuff.* Heaven help the creative children of a compulsive housekeeper̃ They make things, they collect things, they do experiments, and they don't want you to throw them away. Even worse, they don't want you to move something they are making, like a bridge of blocks in the middle of the living room floor. I remember telling Johnny, when he was two, to put his blocks away when he got through playing.

"I don't *get* through playing," he said.

You often have to decide which is more important, the development of your child's gifts, or what the neighbors will think. This takes us back to that important Rule Three: you must not be too concerned about what other people think, and you must not teach your child to knuckle under to public opinion except in matters of minor importance. In those exceptions, you should certainly teach him to be courteous and kind.

What else can parents do? Certainly parents should talk to and *listen to* their children, and try to answer their multitudinous questions; read to them before they can read, afterwards providing books and encyclopedias (get them library cards); take them to operas, plays, museums, concerts, on nature walks; teach them what you as parents have to offer, such as taking an engine apart or playing the piano; see that they have lessons in other areas that interest them BUT DON'T FILL UP ALL THEIR TIME. Gifted people of all ages have a great need of time for themselves, alone.

The chief problem is obvious. What about the parents who can't afford concerts and encyclopedias, who don't have a second car for the mother to transport the child to the special school? What about parents who are too busy or not interested?

This is why we must do more for the "deprived" gifted—rich or poor—and why they are harder to identify in the first place. There are no easy solutions, but this is why federal funds for the "disadvantaged" are more plentiful now that our country has become conscious of this inequity; *every school district should take advantage of these funds.* The Report to Congress tells us that very few are doing so. Parents can speak through the PTA or their Gifted Association or their congressman, or the Board of Education to get these funds and use them.

Professors Thomas and Crescimbeni, authorities we have quoted in the controversies at the beginning of some chapters, say that a vocal parent group demanding that the Board of Education do more for the gifted children in the community cannot be ignored. Unfortunately, school principals find it very hard to ignore the parents who call up and complain about new programs they don't like. So if your child is in a special program you like, let the principal know.

It would be a kindness if parents who are providing transportation for a child of their own to a special gifted program would also pick up one or two children who couldn't otherwise go. This would help not only the child who is deprived of cultural and/or material advantages but also their own children who are often deprived of chances to be thoughtful of the needs of others. Studies have shown that the "elite" are *more* naturally compassionate, more conscious of social injustices, than the average person, but too many "rich kids" seldom have a chance to develop this valuable trait. We don't realize how selfishness, or at least self-centeredness, can dominate the lives of the well-to-do. The experience of "busing" a gifted friend from another community to a special school would be more worthwhile than ballet lessons or a season ticket to the opera; perhaps it would also be possible to take the friend along to the opera.

Most parents are delighted when their children are selected for special programs, or when acceleration is suggested by the school, but many others are not. The average-ability parent of a good student may worry because he cannot trust anything new; it is the gifted who are, by and large, the innovators.

In the interest of helping all gifted as well as their own, parents can take an active role in treating a local parent association for the gifted in their community. Or, by joining an existing one and lending strength and time to make it more effective. The Federal Study of Gifted and Talented in 1969 and the subsequent 1971 *Report of Congress* served as the impetus, not only for action in schools on behalf of gifted students, but also for action on the part of parents of gifted children. Parent associations have sprung up throughout the country and serve as strong advocates for the gifted. In states such as California and Connecticut, parents are a very effective lobby and thereby participate directly in molding legislation. The thrust of these groups is to form a strong base of advocacy in order to insure that planning for gifted individuals becomes a part of the planning for the education of all children. Today the real power for changes in education lies with the parents.

Should parents accept the recommendation of the school for his child's education? Ideally, educator and parent work together in planning a child's education, but when the parent finds himself in the dilemma I faced when I had to decide between two doctors, it must be remembered that educators—like doctors—may recommend different things! So at least *sometimes* the parent—who knows the child better than anyone else should refuse to accept the school's opinions.

My husband and I battled our children's way through grade school by insisting on an occasional skipped grade when we knew they already knew everything in that grade; no other plan was offered for gifted children in our small town. We had both skipped grades in our childhoods with good results, and we are in a position to say, now that our children are through school, that it also worked out well for them. Frea graduated first in her high school class, completed college *magna cum laude,* and is now happily married, has five children *and* a career. Sheila Mary—her own idea—went from her junior year in high school to college when that opportunity was first extended.

"But you'll miss your senior year in high school!" I protested. That was the year I had the most fun, what with being in love and all the extracurricular activities.

"I'll have fun in college," she said, and she did. Now, she is married, with four children, and works mornings as a teachers' aide, while they are in school.

As for Johnny, who was a senior in high school when he died, moving ahead seemed to give him two extra years of living and learning "to his fullest capacity." And he lived four years longer than the doctors thought he possibly could.

David, the one who went through all the grades, was the one who said, when he got his Ph.D., "I've hated school ever since I was six."

On the other hand, if you want to hear of cases of people who wish they had not skipped, you will find letters in Louise Bates Ames's *Is Your Child in the Wrong Grade?*

I do not pretend to be an authority on what someone else should do, but I do believe parents have rights regarding the education of their children which are often high-handedly ignored. Dr. William Vassar of Connecticut, one of the most dedicated and influential people in gifted education, said in a talk in San Diego that parents do have "the right of refusal." Mrs. Ames, who believes in grouping children by ability but not in acceleration, says parents have the right to insist that their children remain in a grade if they are not ready for the next grade, but not the right to ask that they be put in a higher grade.

How then can parents decide when to follow the school's recommendation for a gifted child and when not to? If the school wants to do something special for your child because they have given him tests and observed his school behavior then I think by all means you should cooperate in every way you can, even if it's something new that you don't know as much about as they do. While some special programs have faults that are ironed out during experimentation, I have been visiting innovative schools and pilot programs for three years now, and I have yet to see one that wasn't better (for gifted or any other children) than the egg-crate classrooms I went to and my children went to.

And you can always ask the kids!

It is when a school wants to hold a child back, to ignore his gifts, to keep him from learning, that you must try to do something for him yourself, provided of course that you are sure he is gifted, and that you are not merely ambitious for him. Such parents do exist, and they are a pain in the neck to their own children as well as to the schools. But many parents are called ambitious when in fact they are simply standing up for their children's right to the freedom to learn.

If a school system refuses to do anything at all for gifted children, and also has a blanket rule that NO child shall EVER be allowed to skip a grade, and you can't budge them in this decision, then I suggest that you move!

One last point (for emphasis): Be careful not to make a gifted child your Life Work—it's *his* life! Or hers . . .

SPECIAL INTEREST REFERENCES:

Kaufman, Felice. *Your Gifted Child and You*. Reston, Virginia: Council for Exceptional Children, 1976. A well-written, readable book written expressly for parents and well laced with case studies and anecdotes which will "hit home" for many parents.

Dept, J. L., and Martinson, R. A. *The Gifted and Talented: A Handbook for Parents.* Ventura, California: Office of the Ventura County Superintendent of Schools, 1975. Another fine book for parents. Written by two world-renowned authorities on education of the gifted.

A bibliography of "Thought Provoking Books for Good Readers" is useful as families plan together their home reading activities and trips to the library. Copies can be obtained by writing to Advanced Programs Office, Palo Alto Unified School District, 25 Churchill Avenue, Palo Alto, California 94306. Cost: $1.00.

Conclusions
Where Are We?
What Is Being Done?
What Remains to Be Done?

The case rests; the yeas and nays have been heard. What can one make of the controversy? A thoughtful examination and evaluation of the differing points of view and the literature accompanying each appears to yield certain "truths." They are as follows:

1. Children are treasures, and this includes the gifted. Kate Hoover Calfee, kindergarten teacher par excellence, wrote in the Spring issue of the California Association of the Gifted *Communicator*, "Gifted children are treasures to be encouraged in their uniqueness, not machines to be tuned to their highest R.P.M.'s." To know the fine line between challenge and push is a characteristic of fine teachers. We know that quantity is not quality. We know that very bright youngsters learn to read earlier than other children and with greater ease; they question authority; they recall information readily; generalize easily; do inductive as well as deductive thinking; memorize easily, and so on. Lists of characteristics of gifted behavior abound, or you could make your own. But we also know that these treasures need time to reflect, to process experiences and ideas, and that they have a right to creative and inspirational teaching.

2. We also know of the dangers of generalizations. All gifted people are not alike. Their packaging not only varies in size, weight, color, and shape, but also in the nature of their giftedness. A brilliant mathematician may be a nonreader of nonmathematical materials, the poet may have trouble doing everyday computations, the class

star may need his younger sister to tie his shoes. The gifted are as different from each other as are the individuals in any other group. They, as well as all children, should be taught as individuals. We must be alert to the IQ-worship trap; an IQ is but one thread that makes up the total fabric that is the child.

3. The influence of parents in the life of a child is awesome. The investment of time and energy in the early years of a child's life yields lifelong dividends. An introduction to the wonders and mysteries of the world is most effectively accomplished by families as they plan and do things together. Reading to a child, listening to him, responding to his questions [if there are answers, and if not, "I don't know—let's look it up" is perfectly appropriate], and providing the dignity for his role as a child and learner are essential elements in parenting of gifted children.

4. What about the school environment, the teacher, and the "stuff" of instruction? How children are grouped to learn must be a function of the physical resources of a school—there may not be many options, and moreover, learning can take place in barns, and on the proverbial log. The teacher, however, is crucial. The most effective teachers of the gifted children have been described by parents and the students themselves as ones who listen, have high but clear expectations, are fair, have a sense of humor, don't put kids down or do other demeaning things to anyone, and are nonjudgmental. A fifth-grade, highly gifted child said that he likes a teacher who remembers what it was like to be a child.

5. The stuff of instruction is crucial. The curriculum must be as varied and as vast as resources will allow. A lead must be taken from each child—his interests and his ability to learn—as planning occurs. The community, the world around, must be the school. Fortunately, the notion of the textbook as the primary source of instruction is outmoded. Rigor and discipline must be a part of the learning experience too. Inveterate dabblers do neither themselves nor anyone else any good. But work can be fun and rewarding to teacher and student alike.

We owe a debt of gratitude to many pioneers and devoted workers in the area of teaching and understanding the gifted. It would be hard to try to mention them all. In any book on the gifted, however, the author would be negligent if reference to some who have made significant contributions were not made. Currently, Dr. John Curtis Gowan of California and Dr. E. Paul Torrance of Georgia are our senior senators. Their research work and their years spent in inspiring and encouraging teachers of the gifted have had great impact on where we are today in gifted education. Some of their publications are listed in the bibliography of this book, while others are readily available in college and university libraries. The influence of Dr. James Gallagher of Duke University in North Carolina is apparent throughout this country inasmuch as his text with its clear, specific observations and suggestions is required reading for most classes concerned about teaching gifted students. Joe Khatena, Don Treffinger of the Buffalo Institute of Creative Study, Frank Williams of Oregon, and Joe Renzulli of the University of Connecticut are continuing to offer guidance as we consider the relationship between giftedness and creativity.

California pioneers Ruth Martinson and Paul Plowman helped clarify early issues and continue to provide guidance. Bill Vassar, Consultant for the Gifted in the State Department of Education in Connecticut, was, and continues to be, a powerful advocate for the gifted. He was smart enough in the early years of gifted education to include the gifted in the special education program in his state. As a result, separate lobbies for the gifted do not exist, all exceptionalities are provided for within the same legislation. Dr. Vassar continues to produce fine curriculum materials and conduct in-service training for administrators and teachers. Two women long active in teaching and teacher education will be receiving national attention soon through the publication of their books. Dr. Joanne Rand Whitmore, currently of the George Peabody College for Teachers and previously a teacher in California, has had a special interest in the gifted underachiever; she writes about this in a book to be available in the fall of 1979. A book by Dr. Barbara Clark of California State University at Los Angeles, who led the California battle for special credentials for teachers of the gifted, will also be available late in 1979.

Many persons of eminence and with impressive credentials and degrees have contributed to the gifted child movement over the past twenty-five years. Persons of lesser eminence and fewer credentials have also had impact — namely the teachers and administrators who on a daily basis have taught the children and dealt with the various school communities that challenged "special education" for the gifted. Unfortunately, the struggle continues; it is the brave and secure teacher [tenure is not all bad] who dares to speak out for the gifted.

"The child with a high IQ who fares poorly in class, the creative child who becomes listless in the daily round of school activities, the child whose special gifts go unglimpsed or ignored—such children are familiar to parents, teachers, and administrators; but far less familiar are ways to help them." So reads the introduction to the April 1978 *Federal Aid Report*, published by Croft NEI. The topic of this issue, "How to Avoid Stressing the Wrong Things When You're Writing a Proposal for a Grant for the Gifted and Talented," addresses itself to the amount of Federal support available to state departments, school districts, leadership training institutes, interns, graduate students, and contractors. It does a precise job of defining gifted and talented and provides clues to success in applying for the Federal money. Federal money, however, is far from abundant. The total was $2.56 million for the year 1978—hardly enough to provide for the 2.5 million population of gifted and talented children in this country (a dollar per scholar!). Furthermore, funding for 1979 is uncertain since the legislation that has provided the gifted and talented money will be expiring.

The *Federal Aid Report* indicates that Dr. Dorothy Sisk, Director of the program, "is putting in a request, or planning on funding at about the same level. However, unless the program is reauthorized or renewed, there will be no legislation. So that to say that there will be funding for 1979 is hopeful—and it's speculative—but it very likely will come to pass." An unstable dollar behind programs for the gifted is not a very comfortable condition! The present funding includes thirty state departments of education and a "number of local education agency projects." States reporting the largest utilization of Federal funds in 1976-1978 are Texas, Pennsylvania, Virginia, New York, Connecticut, Maryland, Wisconsin, North Carolina, Mississippi, and Wyoming.

The commitment of individual states to the gifted and talented effort is almost as varied as the number of states. Legislation in California calls for $100 per year per child to be available in special monies to provide for the academically gifted who are in qualitatively different programs. To date, the $100 feature of the legislation has yet to become a fact. Pro-ration has existed since the inception of the legislation in 1961. When pro-ration was declared illegal in 1975 the decision was made to cut back by 25% the number of students who could be served in order to bring the student population in line with the dollar available. This action eliminated the participation of many gifted children in the program. Then, to dilute further the opportunities for these children, the success of the Jarvis-Gann property tax limitation in 1978 resulted in an additional 10% cutback in funds! "Because of funding uncertainties, the program could be eliminated next year," said Sieg F. Efken, chief administrator of gifted programs in the state Department of Education, in the *San Jose Mercury News*, August 13, 1978. "The door could be slammed shut rather than closed slowly, particularly as the competition for the state dollar continues. There's a strong move afoot to get as many as 300,000 parents of gifted children to lobby for continuation of this state-funded categorical program", he said. "I believe it's going to take a hell of an effort. But I don't believe we'll lose it."

The picture in the state where the largest number of identified gifted live is not all rosy. The 1976-1977 estimate of gifted and talented within the total state student population was 197,000; 4.5% of this total school population was reported as gifted and receiving services.

In North Carolina, 3.3% of its total school population is identified and served as gifted; Minnesota reports 2.8%; Nebraska, 2.7%; Maryland, 2.3%; and Virginia, 2.3%. Sixteen states allocated no funds for gifted and talented; none of these states received Federal funding.

In 1977 each state and territory was asked to describe and document the existence of state policy governing the education of gifted and talented children for a Council for Exceptional Children study. Twenty-seven states [53%] have both statutes and administrative policy documents. Six states [12%] have statutes but no written regulations or guidelines. Ten states [20%] have administrative policies but no statutes. Eight states [16%] have neither statutes nor administrative policy.

An important indicator of a state's commitment to educational programs for the gifted and talented is the amount of staff time it invests in coordination and consultation. As of June 1, 1977, twenty-seven states report that they have at least one person with a full-time professional assignment in the area of gifted and talented education. Four of these twenty-seven states have two full-time persons—Alabama, Illinois, Pennsylvania, Washington; two states have three full-time persons—California, North Carolina.

The above information was gathered from *The Nation's Commitment to the Education of Gifted and Talented Children and Youth* [1978], A Summary of Findings from a 1977 Survey of States and Territories, Prepared for the United States Office of Education, Office of Gifted and Talented, by the Council for Exceptional Children, 1920 Association Drive, Reston, Virginia 22091. This fine resource book is available for $6.50 at the above address. If your interest is in a detailed analysis of the nation's condition vis-a-vis the gifted, this is the reference for you. Caution: Figures or indications of sums of money spent must not be confused with the actual quality of programs. One can assume that opportunity for quality is available with more resources, but actual quality can best be determined by asking a different set of questions.

We've seen progress since the Terman days; we've seen progress since the Sputnik days; we've seen progress since the 1971 *Report to Congress*. But has it been enough or in the right direction? What are the problems or needs that remain standing in the way of appropriate education for the gifted of our country?

1. Community backing. This has always been a problem. We need to boost the numbers of interested citizens if we are to make permanent gains in this effort.

2. Administrative backing. You can not have a program without the support of the principal of the school, the supervisor of the principal, or the superintendent and the local Board of Education. The principal is given his authority by his supervisors and wields a great deal of power in our system of education. That power should be a good thing since communities differ in their needs and resources, and direction by a distant agency would be intolerable to most Americans. This means, however, that while a principal can provide, or appoint, the creative leadership necessary for outstanding new programs, he or she can also smother any sparks of enthusiasm directed toward improving "the way it's always been

done." And principals are extremely sensitive to parents, for which we can blame — or thank? — a gifted guy named Alexander Graham Bell, who made the telephone possible.

3. Teachers sympathetic to bright students and prepared to teach them in better ways. This must continue to be a top priority. In-service help for teachers has been provided in many states through their state or Federal money. Dr. Paul Plowman, Consultant for Gifted in California, summarized the federal project "Development of Teaching Competencies — Gifted and Talented" as follows: Over 3000 teachers attended one or more of the 92 Federal Project Workshops during 1976-1977. The greatest number of responses to a teacher questionnaire showed an increase in the skills of:

Asking questions that deliberately elicit higher intellectual and/or creative responses from gifted children.

Applying concepts and skills that aid all children.

Differentiating instruction for the gifted.

Applying creative problem-solving, idea generating, critical-thinking, analytical or decision-making skills in non-teaching aspects of life.

If we multiply each teacher who attends training classes by 25-30 or more children, we get some notion of the kind of impact our efforts in this area can have.

4. Dissemination of ideas. Until very recently, states and even school districts struggled alone, with much duplication of effort. Today, states and districts share and must continue to share efforts. Connecticut's Bill Vassar composed fine materials that describe quality programs for gifted; the state of California has published Exemplary Teaching and Curriculum Guides in English, Social Studies, Mathematics, and Music. The Council for Exceptional Children has a clearing house for information and materials on teaching the gifted and talented. Perhaps each state, through its state Association for the Gifted, could assume some responsibility for dissemination of materials within the state and with other state associations. Nueva

Day School in Hillsborough, California, under the talented leader-ship of Jim Olivero and Del Alberti, has developed fine enrichment materials. The annual conference of the National Association for the Gifted, to which all states send representatives, could be an arena for dissemination of information. It could do a great service by forming a Standing Committee whose function would be the dissemination of ideas developed in various parts of the country.

5. Money! This may seem a long way down the list, but there are things money can't buy as well as things you can't have without it. Many gifted students *have* come successfully through our schools, and most of them attribute this to a few outstanding teachers. As far as general funds are concerned, the community has, in the past at least, backed our schools, and superintendents have, on the whole, run them in a businesslike way. Very little though has ever been spent on the gifted; *The Nation's Commitment* document mentioned previously in this chapter supports this contention.

Currently, local communities are not too happy about *anything* that costs extra money, and that is understandable. I'm a taxpayer myself, *and it hurts.*

But why have we only barely begun to tap all the community resources that are available either free or at low cost? For examples, see my *Creative Teaching*, 1971, Chapter 5, "Help from the Com-munity." A book could be written on this subject alone, including in-formation on the use of expert volunteer personnel from business, the arts, and local colleges. A good example is the "schools without buildings" programs (like the Philadelphia Parkway Program), which use community facilities. Initial expenses in such projects should pay off in the long run; individual teachers with initiative often run programs that not only don't cost anything, but even make money, like selling original Christmas cards (one elementary school made and sold 4000) or books of poetry written and illustrated by the kids.

Also, better education for our best students can *save* money. This could come about in several ways already touched on:

1. By *acceleration*, the elementary and secondary education of able students can be accomplished in at least one to three years less time per student. This would save on teachers' salaries, number of classrooms needed, materials, and administrative expenses. Many

studies show that acceleration does not harm pupils or, indeed, that
it is of benefit. Claims that it does harm are based on individual cases
and emotional prejudices, which often stem from the educational
climate of 1930-1950; some authorities include the 1920s. In my husband's and my experience as pupils in the late 1920s in Washington,
D.C. and California, and as parents in the 1940s in Maine, the opposition got worse. But perhaps geography has something to do with
it, too.

2. The better education of more of our outstanding students would
result in their becoming more productive members of our society; as
such they would pay more than the average share of the tax load. As
Ruth Martinson points out in Volume 2 of the Report to Congress
(*Education of the Gifted and Talented*) the difference between
average lifetime high school and fifth-year college income is
$246,000 (Bureau of Census, *Digest of Educational Statistics*, 1970).
The income tax on this difference, in a conservative 25 percent
bracket, would be $61,500.

Yet right now, states with the *best* programs for the gifted spend
little per year per pupil above the regular school program. If we
spend $250 a year, a more reasonable amount which would still be
far less than is spent on the physically handicapped and retarded, the
special education of all the different kinds of gifted students
throughout their entire school career would cost $3000 per pupil (*if*
he attended twelve years,) but this same pupil would (and might not
otherwise) "repay" $61,500 or more in taxes based on increased earn-
ing power.

Having said all this to persuade anyone who cares that much about
money, I must add that what most of us who are fighting for them
really care about is the kids. A truly deserving minority—in all colors.

3. Bored geniuses and undeveloped leaders and creative artists are
potential dropouts, delinquents, criminals, or (at the least) welfare
recipients! All these cost a lot of money and cause a lot of misery.

Education, as almost every outstanding educator since Plato has
said, should above all be aimed at the development of virtue. An ex-
ception would be Machiavelli in his instructions to The Prince, but
he is in such a minority that his name has become synonymous with
"evil."

Plato said, "Education makes good men."

Locke said, "Tis virtue then, direct virtue, which is the hard and valuable part to be aimed at in education."

Many more such quotations could be added, and studies show that gifted children tend to be good, generous, compassionate, and honest. Is an educational system in which such children are held back, frustrated, and deprived of their natural joy in learning and producing going to make them better citizens? And should we continue to waste so much of their valuable time?

A good point often made is that their presence in classrooms with other children is helpful and stimulating. More authorities agree that part of their time may be well-spent in regular classrooms, where they can tutor slower learners to their mutual benefit.

But authorities also agree that gifted, talented, and creative children are stimulating to *each other*, and should spend a substantial part of their time with their true peers. When we talk about "peer groups" and "peer pressure," we tend to assume that children of the same chronological age are peers, since this is the way our schools are arranged. But Funk and Wagnalls *Standard College Dictionary* says *peer* means "an equal, as in natural gifts or in social rank" — a most "undemocratic" definition!

Some of the highly gifted, especially those who live in small towns, succumb to social pressures because they would not have *any* friends otherwise; some simply cannot bring themselves to conform and are lonely and unhappy. Some well-adjusted children, especially if they have understanding parents or teachers, manage to educate and entertain themselves, and maintain their individuality; they may become social leaders as well.

The dissemination of information such as techniques, programs, and available funds for gifted students is also especially needed in the less populated areas. Many of our large cities are not only developing outstanding programs of their own; educators are hopping planes to share ideas with other advanced states and cities. But in too many small towns and rural areas some of the nicest little kids in town are getting a rough deal. If their teachers and school boards have even heard of any new ways of educating good students, they're dead set against them.

These are the children, along with the unrecognized talented and gifted hidden in the ghettoes and slums of the cities, who are most in need of our help. Sometimes, their only advocates are their parents, who get nothing but abuse for their concern.

The gifted in the ghettoes rarely have even these natural advocates. But a natural-born leader is hard to put down. Many people think of all members of poor or deprived minorities as lazy, "shiftless," or unambitious simply because the *average* members of these communities find it hard to rise above their disadvantages. But the gifted want to "move up," to get out of the ghetto. They are not shiftless or unambitious but *hungry* for success. If only we give them a chance.

Unfortunately, colleges that accept any black or brown student on a *nonselective* basis, as some do under the Educational Opportunities Program, may be doing these communities a disservice. It doesn't help anyone's self-image if he fails, and there are too many other minority students who have the qualifications needed for success. We must *find* them, early in their elementary school careers or sooner, and *prepare* them for college if they are academically talented or train them for an art, trade, or skill.

We should "develop total talent," said Joseph Rice, then the Chief of the Bureau of Special Education in California, in his comprehensive 1970 book, *The Gifted*. "Create a talent pool" of children gifted in all the ways there are: mentally superior, highly creative, talented in one of the performing arts, mechanically or physically or socially gifted, or (usually) a combination of these.

"The public has never bought isolation for Terman-type kids," as Connecticut's William Vassar says, "but once you start broadening the concept you get more public support."

The old objection that special education for gifted children is undemocratic may finally be scotched if we find the outstanding members of all communities and *find them as young as they must be found*. The latest estimate discloses that 80 percent of a person's intelligence is developed by age eight. We must provide preschool education for those whose parents can't or won't, and give them the special attention and encouragement they need during their years of compulsory education. We make them go to school presumably to learn. The least we can do is to let them really learn while they are there.

I wish I knew what we could do about the proverbial problem of the otherwise good and kindly Americans whose compassion reaches out to the handicapped but who resent bright children. If we broaden our definition of who is gifted, though, we are going to invade just about every family in the land.

Parents are noted for being proud of their own offspring and I don't think much of any parent who isn't. Somebody else's kids being considered smarter is what seems to be hard to take, so the more parents we get involved by identifying *their* children as outstanding, the more support we will have for gifted education, as Dr. Vassar says.

This new concept is going to run into some opposition, of course, from an old guard accustomed to fighting for the neglected kids with the high IQs; we haven't won our battle for *them* yet, either. But most of today's leaders in the field—Torrance, Gowan, Gallagher,Sato, Vassar, Martinson, Ward, Hermanson, and many more—know that geniuses turn up in the most unlikely backgrounds, and that the IQ tests we've been using are generally better suited to the kids in the high socioeconomic communities. This doesn't mean we haven't found kids with IQs of 200 in all walks of life and at all economic levels. Nor does it mean that we don't still need programs designed especially for the mentally gifted at high cutoff points. Appropriate programs should be devised for all types of giftedness.

Giftedness?

The terms we use are so seldom satisfactory. Gifted kids don't like to be called gifted kids. Obviously, *superior* is out, and so is *elite*, except as a joke, as when they call themselves *weird*. *Able* is stuffy, *smart* is apt to be followed by *aleck*; *bright* isn't quite so bad.

Exceptional would have been passable, but it somehow got identified more with the retarded and handicapped, as a euphemism, and it works well for that purpose. So these other "special" children are still looking for a name.

Why couldn't we use the term *leaders?*

The American people have pretty good feelings about leadership, and it would cover "mentally gifted minors" (MGM is the California acronym), champion athletes, creative artists, or skilled mechanics and craftsmen, as well as political, social, professional, and industrial leaders.

We could have leadership programs rather than gifted programs; kids chosen for them, like officers in extracurricular activities, would be admired rather than resented; age-group pressure would be put to good use rather than used as a weapon to destroy talent and self-confidence.

And *all* children would be motivated to develop any potential talents; the "underachievers," the "average," the "disadvantaged" and the physically or educationally handicapped in addition to those who seem to be born with a golden spoon in their mouths. Indeed, we all know how often a handicapped child will do much more than the one for whom everything comes too easily.

Utopian? No, it is possible. And we are headed in that direction. This is the most hopeful sign of permanent progress in the history of special education for the children who want it most:

The ones who love to learn.

BIBLIOGRAPHY

Abraham, Willard. *Common Sense About Gifted Children.* New York: Harper and Brothers, 1958.

Ames, Louise Bates. *Is Your Child in the Wrong Grade?* New York: Harper & Row, 1967.

Ashton-Warner, Sylvia. *Teacher.* New York: Bantam, 1971.

Barbe, Walter B., ed. *Psychology and Education of the Gifted.* New York: Appleton-Century-Crofts, 1965.

Beadle, Muriel. *A Child's Mind.* New York: Doubleday, 1970.

Beck, Joan. *How to Raise a Brighter Child.* New York: Trident Press, 1967.

Birmingham, John, ed. *Our Time is Now.* New York: Praeger, 1970.

Black, Hillel. *The American Schoolbook.* New York: William Morrow, 1967.

Boorstin, Daniel J. *The Sociology of the Absurd.* New York: Simon & Schuster, 1971.

Brandwein, Paul F. *Teaching Gifted Children Science in Grades One Through Six.* Sacramento: California State Department of Education, 1973.

Bricklin, Barry and Patricia M. *Bright Child—Poor Grades.* New York: Delacorte Press, 1967.

Bridges, Sydney. *Problems of the Gifted Child: I.Q.—150.* New York: Crane-Russak Co., 1974.

Briggs, Dorothy C. *Your Child's Self-Esteem: The Key to Life.* New York: Doubleday, 1975.

Bruch, Catherine B. *Teaching Gifted Children Social Sciences in*

Grades Four Through Six. Sacramento: California State Department of Education, 1971.

Bruner, Jerome S. *The Process of Education*. Cambridge, Mass.: Harvard University Press, 1960.

Burt, Cyril. *The Gifted Child*. New York: John Wiley & Sons, 1975.

Coleman, James S. *et al. Equality of Educational Opportunity*. Washington, D.C.: National Center for Educational Statistics, U.S. Government Printing Office, 1966.

Conant, James B. *The American High School Today*. New York: McGraw-Hill, 1959.

The Comprehensive High School. New York: McGraw-Hill, 1967.

DeHaan, Robert F. *Accelerated Learning Programs*. Washington, D.C. (now in New York): Center for Applied Research in Education, 1963.

Delp, J. L., and Martinson, R. A. *The Gifted and Talented: A Handbook for Parents*. Ventura, Calif.: Office of the Ventura County Superintendent of Schools, 1975.

Dodson, Fitzhugh. *How to Parent*. Los Angeles: Nash Pub. Corp., 1970.

Drews, Elizabeth. *Learning Together*. Englewood Cliffs, N. J.: Prentice-Hall, 1972.

Engelmann, Siegfried, and Therese. *Give Your Child a Superior Mind*. New York: Simon & Shuster, 1966.

Eurich, Alvin C. *Reforming American Education*. New York: Harper & Row, 1969.

ed. *High School 1980: The Shape of the Future in American Secondary Education*. New York: Pitman, 1970.

Evans, E. Belle; Shub, Beth; and Weinstein, Marlene. *Day Care: How to Plan, Develop and Operate a Day Care Center*. Boston, Mass.: Beacon Press, 1971.

Fine, Benjamin. *Your Child and School*. New York: Macmillan, 1965.

— — —.*Underachievers*. New York: E. P. Dutton, 1967.

Freehill, Maurice. *Gifted Children, Their Psychology and Education,* New York: Macmillan, 1961.

Freehill, Maurice and Hauck, Barbara. *The Gifted: Case Studies.* Dubuque, Iowa: Wm. C. Brown, 1972.

Fraiberg, Selma. *Magic Years.* New York: Scribner, 1968.

Gallagher, James J. *The Gifted Child in the Elementary School.* Washington, D.C.: National Education Association, 1959.

Gallagher, James. *Teaching the Gifted Child.* Boston: Allyn & Bacon, 1975 (revised edition).

— — —.*Teaching Gifted Students: A Book of Readings.* Boston: Allyn & Bacon, 1965.

Galton, Francis. *Hereditary Genius: An Inquiry into Its Laws and Consequences.* New York: World Pub. Co., 1962. (Originally published in 1869).

Gardner, John W. *Excellence: Can We Be Equal and Excellent Too?* New York: Harper & Row, 1961.

Gartner, Alan, Kohler, Mary Conway, and Riessman, Frank. *Children Teach Children.* New York: Harper & Row, 1971.

Ginsberg, G. *Is Your Child Gifted?* New York, Simon & Schuster, 1976.

Glasser, William. *Schools Without Failure.* New York: Harper & Row, 1969.

Goertzel, Victor, and Mildred. *Cradles of Eminence.* Boston: Little, Brown, and Company, 1962.

Gowan, John Curtis and Bruch, Catherine B. *The Academically Talented and Guidance.* Boston: Houghton-Mifflin, 1971.

Gowan, John Curtis and Demos, George D. *The Education and Guidance of the Ablest.* Springfield, Ill.: Charles C. Thomas, 1964.

Gowan, John Curtis and Torrance, E. Paul. *Educating the Ablest.* Itasco, Ill.: W. F. Peacock, 1971. (A book of readings including original material also.)

Gowan, J.C.; Khatena, J., and Torrance, E.P. *Educating the Ablest.* (rev. ed.) Itasca, Il. F.E. Peacock, 1979.

Grost, Audrey. *Genius in Residence*. Englewood Cliffs, N. J.: Prentice-Hall, 1970.

Guilford, J. P. *Intelligence and Creativity: Their Educational Implications*. San Diego, Calif.: R. Knapp, 1969.

— — — . *The Nature of Human Intelligence*. New York: McGraw-Hill, 1967.

— — — . *Way Beyond the I.Q.* Buffalo, N. Y. Creative Education Foundation, 1977.

Hawes, Gene R. *Educational Testing for the Millions: What Tests Really Mean for Your Child*. New York: McGraw-Hill, 1964.

Hermanson, David P. and Wright, David C. *Perceptual Change of Student and Staff toward Learning by Participation in a Seminar Program for the Gifted Learner.* A dissertation presented to the Faculty of the Graduate School of Leadership and Human Behavior, United States International University, and printed by the San Diego City Schools, San Diego, California, June 1969.

Hermanson, David P. and Munsey, Cecil. A series of helpful *Working Papers* issued regularly by the San Diego City Schools Secondary Gifted Program, 1971-1972. Examples: *Individualizing Education for Gifted Senior High School Students; Goals and Objectives for the Secondary Gifted Program 1971-1972* (an Ideabook with 108 practical low-cost objectives); *A Conceptual Framework for a High School for Gifted Students*; and *Dimensions of a Secondary Gifted Program.*

Herndon, James. *The Way It Spozed To Be*. New York: Simon & Schuster, 1968.

Hersey, John. *The Child Buyer*. New York: Alfred A. Knopf, 1960.

Highet, Gilbert. *The Art of Teaching*. New York: Alfred A. Knopf, 1969.

Hill, Mary Broderick. *Enrichment Programs for Intellectually Gifted Pupils*. California Project Talent. Sacramento: California State Department of Education, 1969.

Hollingworth, Leta. *Children Above 180 IQ*. New York: World Book Co., 1942.

Holt, John. *How Children Fail*. New York: Pitman, 1964.

— — —.*How Children Learn*. New York: Pitman, 1967.

— — —.*The Underachieving School*. New York: Pitman, 1969.

— — —.*What Do I Do Monday?* New York: E. P. Dutton, 1970.

Howard, Alvin W. and Stoumbis, George C. *The Junior High and Middle Schools*. Scranton, Pa.: International Textbook, 1970.

Kaufman, Bel. *Up the Down Staircase*. Englewood Cliffs, N.J.: Prentice-Hall, 1964.

Kaufman, Felice. *Your Gifted Child and You*. Reston, Virginia: Council for Exceptional Children, 1976.

Khatena, Joe. *The Creatively Gifted Child: Suggestions for Parents and Teachers*. New York: Vantage Press, 1978.

Kohl, Herbert. *Thirty-six Children*. New York: New American Library, 1967.

Kozol, Jonathan. *Death At An Early Age*. Boston: Houghton-Mifflin, 1967.

Lecomte du Noüy, Pierre. *Human Destiny*. New York: Longmans Green, 1947.

Leonard, George. *Education and Ecstasy*. New York: Delacorte Press, 1968.

Lundy, R.; Carey, R.; and Moore, R. *Dimensions of Learning for the Highly Gifted*. Palo Alto, Calif.: Palo Alto Unified School District, 1977.

Lundy, Ruthe. *Follow-up Study of Double Promoted Elementary School Students*. A dissertation presented to the School Administration faculty at California State University, Hayward, 1974.

Marland, Sidney P., Jr. *Education of the Gifted and Talented*. Report to the Congress of the United States by the U.S. Commissioner of Education. Washington, D.C.: Department of Health, Education and Welfare, 1971, 2 vols.

Martinson, Ruth A. *Curriculum Enrichment for the Gifted in Primary Grades*. Englewood Cliffs, N. J.: Prentice-Hall, 1968.

— — —.*The Identification of the Gifted and Talented.* Ventura, Calif.: Office of the Ventura County Superintendent of Schools, 1974.

— — —.See also (under Marland) *Education of the Gifted and Talented, vol. 2*, for her excellent research summary of the field of gifted education.

Montessori, Maria. *The Montessori Method.* New York: Schocken Books, 1964 (first published in English, 1912).

— — —.*Spontaneous Activity in Education.* New York: Schocken Books, 1965 (first published in 1917).

Munsey, Cecil, and Owenita Sanderlin. *Resource Directory For Teachers of Secondary Gifted.* San Diego City Schools, 1973-1974.

Piaget, Jean. *The Psychology of Intelligence.* Totowa, N. J.: Littlefield, Adams, 1960.

— — —.*Science of Education and the Psychology of The Child*, translated from the French by Derek Coltman. New York: Grossman Publishers, 1970; Paris: Editions Noel, 1969.

Pines, Maya. *Revolution in Learning.* New York: Harper & Row, 1966.

Plowman, Paul D., and Rice, Joseph P. *Final Report: California Project Talent*, Publication No. 6. Sacramento: California State Department of Education, 1969.

Postman, Neil, and Weingartner, Charles. *Teaching as a Subversive Activity.* New York: Delacorte Press, 1969.

— — —.*The Soft Revolution.* New York: Delacorte Press, 1971.

Rice, Joseph P. *The Gifted, Developing Total Talent.* Springfield, Ill.: Charles C. Thomas, 1970.

Riessman, Frank and Hermine I. Popper. *Up From Poverty.* New York: Harper & Row, 1968.

Robb, Mel H. *Teacher Assistants, a Blueprint for a Successful Volunteer-Aide Program.* Columbus, Ohio: Charles E. Merrill, 1969.

Rosenthal, Robert, and Jacobson, Lenore. *Pygmalion in the Classroom.* New York: Holt, Rinehart and Winston, 1968.

Russell, Bertrand. *Education and the Good Life.* New York: Liveright, 1926. Copyright ® 1954 by Bertrand Russell.

Sanderlin, Owenita. *Creative Teaching.* New York: A. S. Barnes, 1971.

———.*Johnny.* New York: A. S. Barnes, 1968.

Seagoe, May V. *Terman and the Gifted.* Los Altos, Calif.: Wm. Kaufmann, 1975.

Sharp, Evelyn. *Thinking Is Child's Play.* New York: E. P. Dutton, 1969.

Silberman, Charles E. *Crisis in the Classroom.* New York: Random House, 1970.

Sisk, Dorothy. *Teaching Gifted Children.* Developed in conjunction with Federal Grant, Title IV, Section 505. Circa 1975.

Stanley, J. C.; George, W. C.; and Solano, C. H., eds. *The Gifted and the Creative: a Fifty Year Perspective.* Baltimore, Maryland: Johns Hopkins University Press, 1978.

Strang, Ruth M. *Helping Your Gifted Child.* New York: E. P. Dutton, 1960.

Sumption, Merle E. *Three Hundred Gifted Children.* Yonkers on Hudson, New York: World Book Co., 1941.

Terman, Lewis M., *et. al. Genetic Studies of Genius.* vol. 1, *Mental and Physical Traits of a Thousand Gifted Children,* 1926; vol. 2, *The Early Mental Traits of Three Hundred Geniuses,* 1926; vol. 3, *The Promise of Youth, Follow-up Studies of a Thousand Gifted Children,* 1930; vol. 4 (with Melita Oden), *The Gifted Child Grows Up,* 1947; vol. 5 (with Melita Oden), *The Gifted Group at Mid-Life, 35 Years Follow-up of a Superior Group,* 1959. Stanford, California: Stanford University Press.

Thomas, George and Crescimbeni, Joseph. *Guiding the Gifted Child.* New York: Random House, 1966.

Torrance, E. Paul. *Gifted Children in the Classroom.* New York: Macmillan, 1965.

———.*Guiding Creative Talent.* Englewood Cliffs, N. J.: Prentice-Hall, 1962.

— — —.ed. *Talent and Education*. Minneapolis, Minn.: University of Minnesota Press, 1960.

— — —.*Torrance Tests of Creative Thinking*. Princeton, N. J.: Personnel Press, 1966.

Vassar, W. G. *Conn-Cept*. Connecticut: State Department of Education, 1976.

Vernon, Philip, ed. *Creativity*. Baltimore, Maryland: Penguin, 1970.

Vernon, Philip. *Intelligence and Cultural Environment*. Scranton, Pa.: Barnes & Noble, 1972.

Vernon, Philip; Adamson, Georgina; and Vernon, Dorothy. *The Psychology and Education of Gifted Children*. London: Metheun & Co., 1977.

Weber, Lillian. *The English Infant School and Informal Education*. Englewood Cliffs, N. J.: Prentice-Hall, 1971.

Weinstein, Gerald and Fantini, Mario D., eds. *Toward Humanistic Education: A Curriculum of Affect*. New York: Praeger, 1970.

White House Conference on Child Health and Protection. *Special Education—the Handicapped and the Gifted*, Report of the Committee on Special Classes, Charles Scott Berry, Chairman, New York: Century Co., 1930. (Interesting to compare to 1971 Report to Congress, *Education of the Gifted and Talented*.)

Witty, Paul, ed. *The Gifted Child*. American Association for Gifted Children. Boston, Mass.: D. C. Heath, 1951.

Wright, Betty Atwell. *Teacher Aides to the Rescue*. New York: John Day, 1969.

Magazine Articles

Asbell, Bernard. "Helping Children to Grow Up Smart." *Redbook*, July 1970.

Bish, Charles, ed. "What's New in Education for the Gifted?" *Accent on Talent*, vol. 2. Washington, D.C.: National Education Association, 1968.

Bruch, C. B. "Modifications of Procedures for Identifying Disadvantaged Gifted." *The Gifted Child Quarterly*, 1971.

Calfee, Kate. "Teaching the Young and Gifted." *Communicator*, California Association for the Gifted, Spring 1978.

DeMott, Benjamin. Review of Herndon's *How to Survive in Our Native Land*. *Saturday Review*, September 18, 1971.

Glatthorn, Allan J. and Ferderbar, J. F. "Independent Study—for *All* Students." *Phi Delta Kappan*, March 1966.

Gold, Marvin. "Kentucky's Lincoln School for Disadvantaged Gifted Youngsters." In Gowan and Torrance, *Educating the Ablest*, 1971.

Goodlad, John I. "Meeting Children Where They Are." *Saturday Review*, March 20, 1965.

— — —."The Schools *vs.* Education." *Saturday Review*, April 19, 1969.

Gowan, John C., "Issues in the Education of Disadvantaged Gifted Children." *The Gifted Child Quarterly*, 1968.

Gowan, John C. and Bruch, Catherine. "What Makes a Creative Person a Creative Teacher?" *The Gifted Child Quarterly 2*, 1967.

Hardy, Joyce. "When Is a Gift Not a Gift?" *California School Boards Association Journal*, June 1978.

Herrnstein, Richard. "IQ." *Atlantic Monthly*, September 1971.

Hersey, John. "Connecticut's Committee for the Gifted." *Educational Leadership*, January 1956.

Honzik, Marjorie P.; McFarlene, Jean W.; and Allen, Lucile. "The Stability of Mental Test Performance Between Two and Eighteen Years." *The Journal of Experimental Psychology 17* (1948).

Illich, Ivan. "The Alternative to Schooling." *Saturday Review*, June 19, 1971.

Javits, Jacob (Senator). In the *Congressional Record*, January 28, 1969.

Jencks, Christopher. "Intelligence and Race." *The New Republic*, September 13, 1969.

Jensen, Arthur R. "How Much Can We Boost IQ and Scholastic Achievement?" *Harvard Educational Review 39* (Winter 1969): 1-123.

Martinson, Ruth; Hermanson, David; and Banks, George. "An Independent Study-Seminar Program for the Gifted." *Exceptional Children*, January 1972.

McLuhan, Marshall. "Electronics and the Psychic Dropout." In *This Book Is About Schools* (a compilation of articles from *This Magazine is About Schools*). New York: Random House, 1970.

McPartland, James. "Should We Give Up on School Desegregation?" *The Johns Hopkins Magazine*, April 1970.

Meeker, Mary N. "Identifying Potential Giftedness." *NASSP Bulletin*, December 1971.

Munsey, Cecil. "Some Don't Have 'Em." *Programs for the Gifted Bulletin*, San Diego City Schools, San Diego, California, Spring 1971.

Raspberry, William. "What About Elitist High Schools?" *Today's Education*, January-February 1976.

Renzulli, Joseph S. "Designing an Instrument for Evaluating Programs of Differential Education for the Gifted." In *The Gifted: CEC Selected Convention Papers*. Washington, D.C.: Council for Exceptional Children, National Education Association, 1967.

Sanderlin, Owenita. "The Wonderful Age of Four." *Parents' Magazine*, December 1958.

Sebesta, Sam. "My Son the Linguist and Reader." *Elementary English Journal*, February 1968.

Spock, Benjamin. "Why I Don't Believe in Speeding Up Primary Education." *Redbook*, October 1965.

Torrance, E. Paul. "Creativity and its Educational Implications for the Gifted." *The Gifted Child Quarterly 12*, 1968.

— — —.In "What's New in Education for the Gifted?" See Bish, Charles, 1968.

Trump, J. Lloyd, and Georgiades, William. "Doing Better With What You Have." A pamphlet reprinted from *The Bulletin of the NASSP*, May 1970.

Tunney, John V. (Senator). "How Smart Do You Want Your Child To Be?" *McCall's*, October 1970.

Whitmire, Janet. "The Independent Study Program at Melbourne High." *Phi Delta Kappan*, September 1965.

Witty, Paul. "Intra-Race Testing and Negro Intelligence." *Journal of Psychology 1* (1936): 179-192.

Zaslow, E. M. "Talent in the Ghetto." *American Education*, March 1967.

Specialty Journals

California School Boards Association Journal. The entire June 1978 issue is devoted to gifted education in California.

The Gifted Child Quarterly. Published by the National Association for Gifted Children, 217 Gregory Drive, Hot Springs, Arkansas 71901.

The Journal of Creative Behavior. Bishop Hall, SUNY, 1300 Elmwood Avenue, Buffalo, New York 14222.

The National Elementary Principal. The February 1972 issue is an outstanding one, specializing in the education of the gifted and talented. It contains much up-to-date information.

Today's Education. January-February 1970 has a special feature on the gifted and talented.

Miscellaneous

"Answers to Frequently Asked Questions About Gifted Education in California." Prepared by the California Association for the Gifted, c/o D. K. Duncan, Office of the Los Angeles County Superintendent of Schools, 9300 E. Imperial Highway, Downey, California 90242.

Gardner, John. "The Anti-Leadership Vaccine." Reprinted from the 1965 Annual Report of the Carnegie Corporation of New York, 589 Fifth Avenue, New York 10017. Gardner believes we are immunizing our most gifted young people against any tendencies to leadership. He describes how the vaccine is administered.

Mentally Gifted Minors Program Models. Published in 1976 by the California Association for the Gifted, c/o D. K. Duncan, Office of the Los Angeles County Superintendent of Schools, 9300 E. Imperial Highway, Downey, California 90242.

Plowman, Paul. "Gifted Child Education and Talent Development Checklist." Revised 1977. California State Department of Education, 721 Capitol Mall, Sacramento, California 95814.

RIF—Reading Is Fun-damental. Margaret McNamara's give-a-book program for motivation of the disadvantaged. Smithsonian Institute, Washington, D.C. 20560, will send information.

"Thought Provoking Books for Good Readers." An annotated bibliography for the child with an insatiable appetite for books. Send $1.00 to the Palo Alto Unified School District, Advanced Programs Office, 25 Churchill Avenue, Palo Alto, California 94306.

Tyack, David. "Compulsory Schooling: Where Did It Come From, Where Is It Going?" *Carnegie Quarterly*, Winter 1977.

"Where the Money Is." A very clear guide to available federal funds published in *American Education* annually, and distributed as a reprint from Superintendent of Documents, U. S. Government Printing Office, Washington, D. C. 20402. $.20 per copy.

Gifted Organizations

American Association for the Gifted, 15 Gramercy Park, New York, New York 10003.

The Association for the Gifted (TAG), a division of The Council for Exceptional Children, 1411 South Jefferson Davis Highway, Arlington, Virginia 22202.

Council of State Directors of Programs for Gifted, California State Department of Education, 721 Capitol Mall, Sacramento, California 95814.

National Association for Gifted Children (NAGC), 217 Gregory

Drive, Hot Springs, Arkansas 71901. John Gowan, Executive Director.

U.S. Office of Education, Office of Gifted and Talented Education, Room 2100, ROB-3, 7th and D Streets, S.W., Washington, D.C. 20202. Dorothy Sisk, Director.

England: The National Association for Gifted Children, 27 John Adam Street, London, W.C.2, England.

World Council for Gifted and Talented, P.O. Box 41/3428, Tehran, Iran. Iraj Broomand, Executive Committee Chairman.

The World Council, the newest organization concerning itself with the education of gifted individuals, has identified for itself the following objectives:

1. To focus world attention on gifted children and their valuable potential contribution to the benefit of mankind.

2. To explore the nature of their talents and resultant problems in childhood and adolescence.

3. To create a "climate" of acceptance of gifted children, not as a privileged elite, but as an invaluable global asset.

4. To assemble, for an exchange of ideas and experience, people from all over the world interested in the gifted and talented.

5. To persuade the governments of the world to recognize gifted children as a category for special attention in normal educational programs.

6. To establish means for a continuing world-wide exchange of ideas, experiences, teaching, and teacher-training techniques in respect of gifted children.

Additional information can be obtained from:

Dr. Iraj Broomand (See address above)

Dr. Dorothy Sisk
Dept. of Health, Education and Welfare
Director, Office of the Gifted and Talented
Bureau of Education for the Handicapped
Washington, D.C. 20202

Mr. Dan Bitan
Department for Gifted Children
Ministry of Education and Culture
Jerusalem, Israel

Your State Department of Education, located in the capital of your state. Local school districts can also provide information for interested persons.

Index